Backyard Brickwork
How to build walls, paths, patios and barbecues

Backyard Brickwork

How to build walls, paths, patios and barbecues

Edited by Mike Lawrence

A Garden Way Publishing Book

STOREY

A Garden Way Publishing Book

First published in the US, 1989, by
Garden Way Publishing
Schoolhouse Road, Pownal, Vermont 05261

The name Garden Way Publishing is licensed to
Storey Communications, Inc. by Garden Way, Inc.

Edited by Angela Whittingham
Cover designed by Behram Kapadia
Designed by Jennie Hoare

Library of Congress Cataloging-in-Publication Data

Backyard brickwork.

  Includes index.
  1. Garden structures – Design and construction – Amateurs' manuals.
2. Building, Brick-Amateurs' manuals. I. Lawrence, Mike, 1947-
TH4961.B32 1989   693'.21   89-45218
ISBN 0-88266-567-7
ISBN 0-88266-562-6 (pbk.)

CONTENTS

1. GROUND RULES FOR BACKYARD DESIGN

With bricks, mortar, concrete, paving blocks and other building materials you can achieve wonderful effects in your yard. And if you are prepared for a little hard work you can do it all yourself, achieving professional finishes and saving a great deal of money in the process. All you need to get started is enthusiasm, instruction in basic building techniques, and some exciting ideas to choose from. Backyard Brickwork will give you all of this, but remember, paths, patios, barbecue areas, walls and steps are all permanent structures, so think carefully before getting started. Time spent in planning will be a great investment in the long run, so before beginning, it is wise to consider a few fundamental points about planning and design.

Style

Gardens usually conform to one of three types: formal, informal and those which combine features of both.

The chief characteristic of an informal garden is that flower beds, paths, lawns and walls flow together without rigid dividing lines. This gives a feeling of spaciousness, because the observer does not take in the whole garden at a single glance. The eye is led naturally from one interesting feature to the next. Straight lines are avoided, while slopes and other natural features are emphasized by the use of materials like stone or brick in such a way as to blend naturally with the plants and the rest of the garden. Most gardeners aim for this informal effect.

In a formal garden, everything is laid out with well-defined borders. Pathways and paved areas are laid in straight lines, while the beds and lawns tend to be square or rectangular. The eye is led in a straight line, called the axisline, to a focal point,

The informal yard, in which flower beds, lawns and patios flow together without rigid dividing lines.

such as a fountain or a group of exceptional plants or flowers. The effect is often heightened by features like paths, rows of shrubs, floral borders, terraces or hedges. A garden of this sort takes a good deal of imaginative design to avoid monotony, and also requires regular and thorough maintenance. A formal garden soon looks neglected if the grass is allowed to grow a bit too long, or when the flowers begin to wilt.

The various features of an informal and formal garden can be combined and often with pleasing results, particularly in a fairly large garden. The area closest to the house, for example, may be best suited to formal treatment. Remember, though, that the transition from the one style to the other must be planned carefully to achieve a harmonious whole.

Perspective

Perspective is another important aspect of good garden design. By planning your garden with ingenuity, you can achieve several different effects. A feeling of cosy security can be created, for example, when you look up from a lower level to a slightly raised patio surrounded by a wall. On the other hand, a sense of spaciousness is created when, standing on the patio, you look down onto the rest of the garden spread out below. And when you are relaxing comfortably on a chair or bench under a sun umbrella or shade tree, you enjoy a different atmosphere. Each time you move your position, your mood changes subtly – and the garden looks just a little different.

You can create new perspectives in your garden by using such ploys as raising your patio or lawn on an artificial hillock, with a winding path leading down to the lower area of the garden. Varying levels can be created by bringing in earth from elsewhere, or by digging it out. The easiest way is to combine a bit of each method. Thus, ground that has been removed from one spot can be used to create a raised area elsewhere. And it is not necessary to move mountains. A little step of 250 to 300 mm from one level to another may be all that is needed.

If your garden is sited on a slope, you must decide whether to keep it as a slope, or to terrace it using retaining walls. The first alternative may appear to be the easiest solution, offering a relaxed, natural setting for the rest of the garden. It can, however, be a problem when mowing or if you want flower beds that won't wash away in a heavy rain storm. Remember, too, it is always more difficult to work in a sloping garden.

If you decide on terraces, bear in mind that the rigid line of a straight terrace wall is more suited to a formal yard. A more informal effect is obtained by the use of curving terrace walls, although they are not as easy to lay out or to build.

Paths

Garden paths serve an important design function. They can be used to define and complement lawns, shrubberies and flower beds. They can also be used to lead the eye subtly toward a particular garden feature.

By allowing a winding pathway to disappear behind a hedge, terrace or hillock, you create a feeling of mystery that beckons the visitor to investigate further. The impression that there is more to be discovered round the corner also makes the garden appear bigger than it is in reality.

On the other hand, do not lay footpaths simply for effect. They must have a purpose – must lead to something – or you will simply be wasting your money by chopping the garden into little bits. Remember, too, that it takes extra work to keep the edges of pathways looking neat.

Shape

Just as your garden can be made more interesting by paying attention to perspective in your design, so can shape play an important role. Circles, for example, provide a feeling of harmony and peace. Curves can be used to avoid

monotony. The success of an informal garden depends on how well you manage to combine the lines of the various angles, curves, circles and straight lines. Always be wary of combining too many contrasting shapes, however, as this gives a feeling of turmoil.

Perceptions

Colours, smells, textures, light and shade, temperature and sound, all play an important role in garden design. A good garden titillates all the senses.

When you plan a patio or seating corner to give the best view of your garden, make sure it is positioned to provide shade in summer and sunshine in winter. Provision should also be made for privacy and shelter against the prevailing wind. This can best be provided by a wall, hedge or pergola. If it is not possible to provide one place for both summer and winter, you may be able to create a sitting nook away from the patio, for winter relaxation. A garden that offers pleasure for only six months of the year has been badly designed.

Care should also be taken to prevent unnecessary noise. If your property borders on a busy road, your garden wall should be designed with special care. A high wall is the usual solution, but building regulations – and the claustrophobic feeling that sometimes results from being walled-in – could persuade you otherwise.

Bear in mind that a hole three feet deep is as effective in absorbing noise

as building a wall three feet higher. Just remove the earth parallel and close to the inside of your boundary wall and use the excavated earth in creating new levels elsewhere in the garden. Shrubs, trees and hedges on the street side will also act as effective sound barriers, particularly when combined with a high wall.

When you have eliminated as many unwanted noises as possible, you can introduce your own garden sounds. The building of a pond with its own waterfall is well within the scope of any weekend enthusiast. It gives an immediate focal point to any garden – and the sound of bird-song, the chuckling of running water and even the croaking of frogs, create a feeling of peace that can be attained in no other way. (See building instructions on pages 79-81.)

Another key to good garden design is the way in which the varying colours and textures of stone, brick, concrete and wood are put to use. There is no reason why you should not use cement products in your garden – and there is also no reason why the end result should look unimaginative. (On page 69 you can find out how mortar can be coloured, and on pages 67-68 you will see how the rough texture of various types of natural stones can be used to give concrete a completely different look).

How big?

Must there be plenty of playing space for children or grandchildren? Do you hope to add a swimming pool at a later stage? Are you an enthusiastic gardener who regards gardening as a hobby, or do you prefer a garden that requires the minimum of upkeep? If you don't want to work in your garden, can you afford the services of a regular gardener? Do you plan to build a bigger garage later? These are all important questions to be answered before embarking on garden features that could turn out to be costly mistakes.

As far as the bigger garage and swimming pool are concerned, take care not to place trees or permanent structures on the sites of future structural additions. It's better to plan lawns or flower beds in these places. Also make sure your sandbox, play area or garden swings are positioned where you can easily keep an eye on them.

Minimum maintenance

One other important decision you must make when planning (or re-planning) a garden is how much time you are prepared to spend on maintenance, particularly if you go out to work during the day.

Enthusiastic homeowners recommend that up to 80 per cent of the yard should be devoted to lawn. This is all very well, but it does mean weekends filled with mowing and edging and a host of other tasks to keep the lawn in good condition, including regular watering in dry spells and a constant fight against attacks from weeds and other lawn pests.

On the other hand, a minimum-maintenance garden certainly does not have to compare unfavourably with a traditional garden filled from edge to edge with lawns, flowers, shrubs and other plants. A garden with a minimum of vegetation can be just as colourful and attractive if it is planned with taste.

The amount of time you decide to spend on garden maintenance should be based on the following piece of garden wisdom: Do not plan anything bigger than you are able to maintain on your own – or that the next owner of your house can maintain. The easier it is for him to keep the garden looking good, the sooner he will be persuaded to sign the sales agreement. (Remember, the average house changes owners six times, and the person who buys a house in your suburb is usually in the same income bracket as you – and likely to have the same problems as you.)

The big secret of minimum-maintenance is maximum-paving and plenty of container plants. Arrange the containers in groups or singly on your patio or porch, around your barbecue or pool and allow your house and garden to flow together by placing more containers in your living room, bedrooms, kitchen and even your bathroom. All you need do is water your plants with a watering can once a week and pinch out the occasional weed with your fingers.

Container plants that are strategically placed on an extensive patio are one of the best ways of breaking visual monotony. Also, the variety of concrete pots and trays in which you can plant is wide, as is the range of warm earth colours you can paint them. In addition, you can move the plants about in their containers, keeping them under cover or in a sheltered spot in winter, to give your garden a new show each season.

Bear in mind that square, or cylindrical, containers are well suited to modern houses, and that they come in a variety of sizes and heights that can be grouped together to form effective arrangements. Position the larger containers at the back and the smaller ones in front.

Natural materials like driftwood and

quarry stones can be arranged around the containers, but take care not to overdo it. The end result can look as artificial as pictures on a cake-tin.

Do not use bright colours when painting concrete containers. Terracotta, beige and chocolate brown look best out of doors, but for indoor use you can select a shade to complement your colour scheme. (Special paints are now available, but you can also use acrylic paints, which do not require an undercoat.)

Remember, too, that you can plant a very wide variety of trees and bushes in containers, as they restrict the growth of all trees. Shrubs and climbers do equally well in containers.

It is as well to remember that plants are of minor importance when you are planning a garden. Indeed, one of the greatest mistakes most home owners and gardeners make is to decide first on the plants they want in their gardens, then just

begin gardening instinctively.

The fundamental principle of good garden design is very simple: The plants come very last. The planning of the permanent structures must come first.

'Planning' is always the key; once you have started building, it is difficult and expensive to change your mind because things don't look good or right. Also, you cannot achieve a harmonious whole when the siting of your permanent structure is limited by the position of temporary structures like flower beds, shrubs or even lawns and trees. And to have to dig out lawns and other plants later to make room for a permanent structure is again a waste of time and money.

This is why you must plan a garden very carefully, right from the beginning, by drawing it to scale on paper, indicating the position of every structure, permanent and temporary. This offers another great advantage: paper is patient and cheap. On it you can spend weeks measuring

and fitting and moving things about until you are completely satisfied with the design of your dream garden.

The way to go about measuring your garden and drawing your plans like an expert is described in Chapter 2.

Planning in general

When buying a house most people seem to regard the garden as an appendage that has nothing to do with the house. In most cases the permanent structures that make a garden attractive are never built, because these important improvements must be paid for out of the monthly family budget – and there is never enough left over for such 'luxuries'.

Often it is the second, or third, owner who discovers the potential of the garden and starts bustling about – but, unfortunately, often making the classic mistakes because of lack of money and proper planning.

Every person who buys a new – or old –

house or who plans to redesign his present garden, should bear the following in mind:

☐ Every dollar that you spend on a well-designed garden and outdoor living space is a sound investment. You will get it back in hard cash when you re-sell the house.

☐ Poor workmanship and badly planned permanent structures are a waste of money, time and effort. In other words, whatever you do, do it well.

☐ The days of huge houses with spacious rooms on cheap and equally spacious plots have gone forever. Building costs, land prices and the pressure of modern city lifestyles demand that you make use of every square foot of your property. To plan a city garden merely for its prettiness is a waste. Your garden must be planned to augment the living, entertaining and relaxing area of your home.

☐ Most houses stand like upright matchboxes in the middle of unused

Left: A spot that is sunny all year round. The waterfall is operated by a small pump and provides another important feature: the soothing sound of trickling water.
Above: Plenty of paving and container plants – the main ingredients for a garden that requires minimum maintenance.

outdoor living space. The only way you could integrate such a garden with the indoor living space would be to break out a door or window and install sliding doors. Include the cost of these in your calculations right from the start.

☐ Take care to include the costs of garden improvements in your calculations when you buy an old house or plan a new one. Most gardens remain unimproved

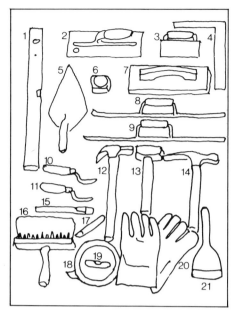

1. Spirit level; 2. plastering trowel; 3. corner trowel; 4. steel square; 5. masonry trowel; 6. tape measure (15 ft); 7. wooden float; 8. square pointing tool; 9. round pointing tool; 10. short, round pointing tool; 11. short, square pointing tool; 12. claw hammer; 13. 2½lb club hammer; 14. brick hammer; 15. chisel; 16. lime (whitewash) brush; 17. wax crayon; 18. nylon builder's line; 19. line level; 20. bricklayer's gloves; 21. wide chisel.
Above right: Concrete stepping stones with a textured surface can be used with striking effect in the garden.

because the costs have been left out in the belief that this will be done later, when more money becomes available. Those days of 'more money' seldom, if ever, dawn for the average family.

☐ Most people hopelessly underestimate the cost of a well-planned garden or outdoor living space. To try to pay the difference from your pocket, even over a period of some years, is not the best solution. Rather, draw up proper plans that comfortably fit your budget. Gardens are wonderfully adaptive and flexible. In this way you will be able to relax in your dream garden much sooner.

Step-by-step
Where do you start when you are planning a new garden or redesigning an existing one?

☐ First, read this book from cover to cover and then decide what kind of garden you want: formal or informal, a show garden filled with flowers and shrubs or a garden that needs the minimum of upkeep.

☐ Then measure your garden and draw a rough sketch plan of everything you would like to have in it. All the necessary information you need to draw up this plan like an expert is provided in Chapter 2.

☐ Then decide on your choice of materials, after reading the chapters on patios, paths, garden walls and so on, and estimate the quantities, using the formulae provided in Chapter 15. Do a cost estimation by telephoning building suppliers, brick suppliers and transport companies and asking for a quotation for the materials you will require.

☐ Then work out how many extra tools you will need to buy, and include this in the total cost of the project. Don't try borrowing from your neighbours. Study the tools list on this page and buy whatever you will need before you begin to build.

☐ When, finally, your plan is complete and you know how much your dream garden will cost, you will have to decide how best to make it a reality. Several factors will play a role here, particularly your own technical ability, your financial position, the amount of free time you have at your disposal and your own personality.

The easy way out
If you are not a practical person and have never had the inclination, or the time, to work with your hands or to learn new skills, turn to page 88. There you will find a list of addresses of various organizations that will put you in touch with good, local architects, draftsmen, landscape architects and builders.

Have your plan redrawn by a draftsman or an architect and ask him or her to draw up a list, in builders' language, specifying the materials as well as the standards to which the work must comply.

These people charge for their services by the hour and you can find out the average rates from the organizations which supplied you with the addresses and telephone numbers. As you will already have done all the measuring and plannng yourself, it will probably cost a lot less than you might expect.

When you have the draftsman's final plan, you must ask at least two reputable builders to give you quotations. If you do not know how to find a good builder, speak to the building inspectors who work for your local authority and ask whether they can recommend anyone.

You can also ask friends who have recently had building done, but make sure these friends know something about building work – because laymen are easily taken for a ride by shoddy builders, without realizing it. This is also the reason why you must not, under any circumstances, simply ask the first builder you find to begin work of any sort on the basis of a verbal agreement, particularly if his quotation seems unusually low and you do not know much about construction work.

Also, under no circumstances should you pay in advance for work that is still to be done. If any problems do arise, you will lose, either in terms of money or in a final result that may have to be demolished.

Once you have a written quotation from two or more reputable builders, go to see your local bank. Take your plan and quotations with you and ask whether they are prepared to lend you the money.

Unless the amount approaches the bank's current assessed valuation of your house, they will in most cases be prepared to grant you either a home improvement loan or a second mortgage secured on the property.

A patio made of bricks laid, without mortar, on a sand base. This is an ideal project for beginners who want to do some brickwork in their gardens.

The do-it-yourself route

If you are practically-inclined, enjoy working with your hands and are not afraid to master the art of building, you can realize your dream garden under your own steam. Here are a few points and tips to bear in mind.

☐ Bricklaying is easy, so easy that any practical person can master it. Anybody who can place one brick on top of or alongside another, with a layer of cement between the two, can obtain a professional result by using the techniques described in this book.

☐ A 'cementless' project, like laying bricks in sand to form a patio or garden path, is one of the best projects for a beginner. It gives you a feel for brickwork – how to obtain a smooth and level surface, how to lay a brick level and how to use your spirit level and straight-edge.

The biggest advantage of a cementless project is that you do not have to worry about mortar becoming hard while you are battling to get into your stride. You also have no worry about messing up the whole area with spilled cement. There is plenty of time to correct your mistakes at a leisurely pace.

☐ When you are ready to build your first planter, step, pillar or terrace, don't just mix up a batch of mortar and start building. First study the bricklaying and other techniques described in this book, then build one of the practice walls shown on pages 33-34.

Then visit a building site in your area to see how the bricklayer sets up his building lines and handles his building tools and spirit level. Now go back and build another practice wall. This time match your style to that of the professional. Build more practice walls (they need only be a foot or two long) until you're quite certain you can keep a wall and its corners plumb.

☐ If you cannot succeed on your own, there is no reason to throw in the towel. Many localities now run adult education classes in all sorts of do-it-yourself subjects. Another answer is to ask a bricklayer to spend a day teaching you (and maybe a friend or two) the basics of bricklaying. It will cost you only a day or two's wages – and you will certainly recover the amount from the money you will save by tackling the project yourself.

Plan all your bricklaying projects carefully and always keep this golden rule in mind: never tackle more than you can manage to complete with patience and good workmanship.

Time

The difference between the price a builder will charge you, and the amount you will save by tackling a project yourself, is time. Your time. How much weekend time are you prepared to devote to a project? How long will it take to complete a given

Once your loan has been approved, get the builder of your choice to sign a contract setting out such details as retention money (the amount held back until such time as the project is completed to your satisfaction), the time in which the project is to be completed and at what stage of the work the first payment will be made. In this way, you can minimize the risk that faces every home owner wishing to have alterations done by unfamiliar builders, landscapers or designers.

If they are good, however, the advantages are obvious. No technical knowledge is required from you, and you have a satisfactory final result in a matter of weeks. All you then need to do is the planting. And as soon as your plants are established, your house is worth much more – sometimes by as much as you spent on improvements, and sometimes by even more. Just ask any real-estate agent how much an attractive outdoor living area adds to the price of a house.

project, using the spare time at your disposal? A month? Six weeks?

Who will help you? Your wife or husband? The children? The neighbour? Or will you have to hire a helper? How much will he cost you, and have you included this sum in your estimate of the total cost of the project?

Are you in a hurry? Do you expect immediate results or are you prepared to go ahead patiently and meticulously, completing the project over an extended period in order to save money?

These questions must be asked, because all too many do-it-yourselfers tackle projects in the false belief that they are going to be dead easy, quick as a wink and ridiculously cheap. This is usually by no means the case – and the sobering reality can make you shy away from a trowel for the rest of your life. When you tackle a building job in your garden, or anywhere else, you are creating a permanent structure with which you will have to live for many years. If you are not prepared to exercise patience and to be meticulous, the results will be skew and crooked and, in all probability, you'll just give up half way.

If there is any chance of this happening with your project, rather go for the first option described in this book: start from scratch by getting an expert to do the work for you correctly, and don't begrudge him his wages for doing it. In your case, it will work out far cheaper in the long run.

But if you are prepared to tackle your garden project systematically, and with the necessary patience, you will be rewarded with one of the greatest senses of satisfaction this rushed modern life has to offer. You create something with your own hands when you build. The time you spend outdoors doesn't seem like work; it is recreation. You know you have done your best and the result looks good. Your richest reward is inner satisfaction – something you cannot buy with mere money.

So avoid the pitfalls into which most do-it-yourselfers fall as a result of their over-enthusiasm. Study your garden plan carefully. Determine which projects fall within your scope, in terms of available time and your own technical ability.

Begin with a simple project like a low terrace wall, a simple step, a pond or a planter. Your proficiency with a trowel will improve as you progress, and eventually you will be capable of tackling the most complicated task with complete confidence.

Do not try to fool yourself into tackling the most difficult project first, simply because it is the most urgent. If the work really is urgent and difficult, rather leave it to a professional builder.

Study the project list shown here. Mark all the projects which you plan to

complete on your own, then arrange them in order of importance. Use this list to select your first project and make certain you have all the necessary tools and materials ready before you begin. Then work out how much time you will need to complete the job. Be generous in your planning.

Say to yourself: I have so much time to complete this little job. Every weekend I shall spend so many hours on it, and I will not allow myself to be hurried or disheartened. And I am going to do it to the very best of my ability, because I do not want to spend the rest of my days staring at a bungled job.

Then forget about all the other work that still has to be done in your garden and elsewhere. Concentrate only on the task ahead, because if you sit and agonize over everything that still has to be done, you will never get started on any of it. By dividing the work systematically into easily-handled stages like this, you will suddenly find new courage. Why not try it: the garden is not the only area in which you can get amazing results this way.

Finally, before you begin, do one more calculation, just for fun. Take a look at the lifestyles of your friends and colleagues.

Calculate how much they spend on jogging and other fitness programs, diets, exercise cycles and all the rest of it, in an effort to keep fit. Now work out how much you will be saving by keeping fit by 'gardening'. Add to this a possible extra five or ten years of life, plus the greater enjoyment of those years by having a healthy body.

Now work out from the beginning, once more, which jobs you will tackle yourself and which you will leave to a builder.

An important part of good planning is drawing up a priority list of projects.

Project List

Project	Very important	Important	Desirable	Builder's costs	Own costs
Barbecue					
Swimming pool					
Garage					
Carport					
Pergola					
Patio					
Garden wall					
Terrace walls					
Drainage					
Container plants					
Paths					
Pond					
Washing line					
Garbage can corner					
Sliding doors					
Awnings					
Play area					
Entertainment area					
Winter corner					
Other:					

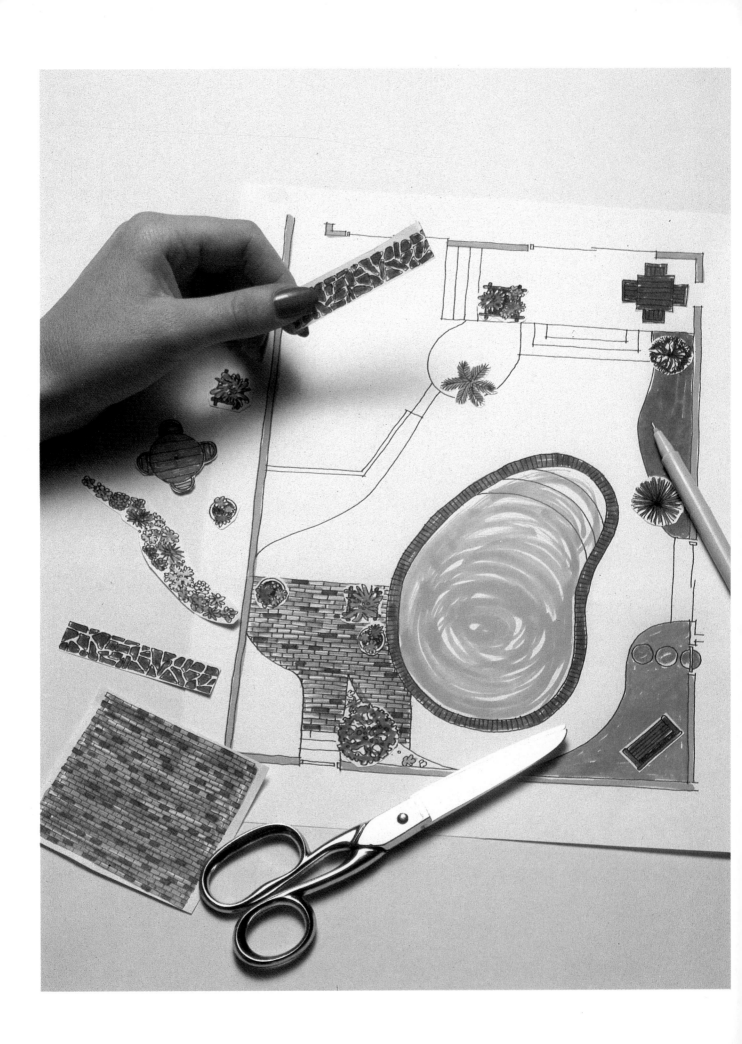

2. PLANNING ON PAPER

The very first requirement of good planning on paper is good ideas. Draw sketches of the attractive things you see in other people's backyards; the well-designed barbecue corner, the bench tucked away under a tree, the pond and its surroundings and the way the bricks are laid in an attractive patio. Take your camera along if you are no good at drawing, or make copies of pretty garden features you find in books.

See where the sun rises and sets in summer and winter and how the shadows move across your property, and indicate this on a rough plan of your yard. Note the places that receive a lot of sunshine – or a little. This will help you to find the best sites for things like your patio.

Always aim to make your yard look as natural as possible. Gnomes and similar creatures occur nowhere in nature. Neither do mailboxes on concrete imitation tree-stumps sprout between flowers.

Don't rush. It is not a waste to spend weeks, or even months, planning something that is going to look good and provide pleasure for a lifetime. And it frees you from one great misery: self-reproach. This usually takes the form of a thought that pops into your head when you are in someone else's yard: 'I wish I'd also thought of that'.

When you have collected enough ideas, reduce all these preferences and vague notions down to a practical design that fits your requirements, your finances and the limitations imposed by the position and size of your plot. The project list on page 15 will help you considerably, not only to decide what permanent structures to build in your yard, but also to establish the priority of each of them. It also provides a chance to calculate costs and to work out which tasks you will undertake on your own and which you will leave to a professional builder.

Measurement and drawing
When you know exactly what you want to do in your yard, you must measure up the whole area around your house. This task will be made considerably easier if you obtain copies of your house's original building and site plans; they are sometimes available from your local municipality (contact the building department first of all).

See that you have the following handy: a set of drawing instruments with all the necessary triangles, a pair of compasses, ruler and a plastic matrix for drawing accurate curves. Sets like this do not cost much, and are available from most good stationers.

Use one or two strong bulldog clips to hold the paper firmly to your drawing board, which can be made cheaply from a piece of hardboard. The only other items you will need are drawing paper, graph paper, tracing paper and a good tape measure about fifteen feet long.

The ground plan
Stick or clamp your graph paper to your drawing board and sketch the outlines of your plot, after first measuring the distances between the house and the boundary lines. Now measure up the positions of every fixed structure such as the house, garage, shed, greenhouse and so on, and mark their positions on the graph paper. The correct scale is obtained by letting each square on the graph paper represent a given size, for example 2 x 2 in. Experiment with various sizes to find one that best suits your circumstances.

Indicate the positions of the windows and sliding doors on your ground plan, so you can plan where to have the best views of the garden. Also indicate any areas where water collects during wet winter weather. No building work should be started until you have eliminated these drainage problems. The way to do this is described for you in Chapter 3.

Also use coloured pens or crayons to indicate where high-lying areas are, as well as the positions of existing trees and their shade areas, as well as their drip circles (the farthest reaches of their branches, where water drips down). Mark other shade and sun patches.

When you have done all this, your ground plan is ready. On this plan you can see at a glance all the existing structures, plus such details as slopes and poorly drained areas and those which receive little sunshine – all in exactly the right places and to scale. With this master plan as a starting point, you are ready to plan your new garden.

The bubble-plan
Take a sheet of clean tracing paper and stick or clip it over your ground plan. Now, with your drawing board tucked under your arm, climb up a ladder to the roof and look down on the world from the top of your garage or house. Draw bubbles, or rings, around the places where you would like to have features such as a patio, a barbecue, a pool, hedges, a terrace, a garden wall, flower beds, and so on. Just draw freehand and use your imagination.

When you've finished your final plan, cut out the symbols and place them in position, to give you a better idea of what the garden will look like when it is completed. Above are some of the symbols you can use: paving, barbecues, one with a table and chairs, and a hedge. A full set of symbols is provided on pages 84-87. Copy the ones you need and colour them in before fitting them into your plan.
Left: With a garden plan you reduce all your ideas to a practical, achievable design.

The drawing board with the ground plan, which shows the existing structures in your yard.
The tracing paper, on which the improvements are indicated, is laid over it.
Far right: the final result – a complete plan on which all the structures are set out accurately.

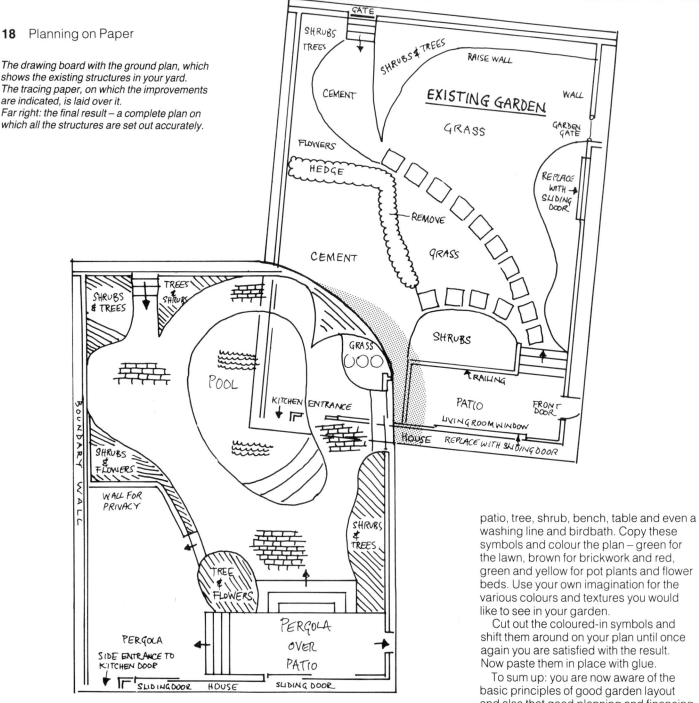

In this way you can build up a three-dimensional image of your garden. When you look down on it from above, you are in a better position to allow the various elements on your drawing board to flow together. At this stage, don't worry about the position of pathways. You limit your creativity if you put them in first. Once the most important features have been positioned, it is much easier to plan pathways.

Climb down from the roof and use this rough sketch to lay out the outlines of the proposed projects on the ground. Use a piece of hose or a thickish rope to indicate the various positions, or hammer pegs into the ground and stretch string between them. Or sprinkle a line of white sand from a tin can to indicate the outlines.

Now take a fresh look from above.

Sketch new outlines if you are not satisfied; shift the hose or rope until you are happy. Now remove your first traced plan and stick a fresh sheet of tracing paper in place on the ground plan. Now draw new bubbles to indicate the new positions. Repeat the whole process until you are perfectly happy with the final result.

Now put away your plans and drawing equipment for at least a week. Re-think everything from the beginning in every spare moment you have. Only when you are completely certain of how your new garden will look should you make your final sketch on tracing paper.

The final plan
Once you are satisfied with your final plan, take a look at pages 84-87. They show the various symbols that represent a lawn,

patio, tree, shrub, bench, table and even a washing line and birdbath. Copy these symbols and colour the plan – green for the lawn, brown for brickwork and red, green and yellow for pot plants and flower beds. Use your own imagination for the various colours and textures you would like to see in your garden.

Cut out the coloured-in symbols and shift them around on your plan until once again you are satisfied with the result. Now paste them in place with glue.

To sum up: you are now aware of the basic principles of good garden layout and also that good planning and financing are necessary if you want to succeed. You have learned not to attempt things that are beyond your capabilities, that a garden should create extra living space, that garden improvements increase the value of your house, that botched-up work will earn you nothing, and that every project should be tackled systematically according to a list of priorities. You have also learned how to collect ideas and to use your own creativity, and how to convert those vague ideas of a dream garden into practical, useable plans.

Building regulations
Building approval is not generally needed for backyard construction work, but could apply to large structures such as swimming pool enclosures. If in doubt, check with your local authority.

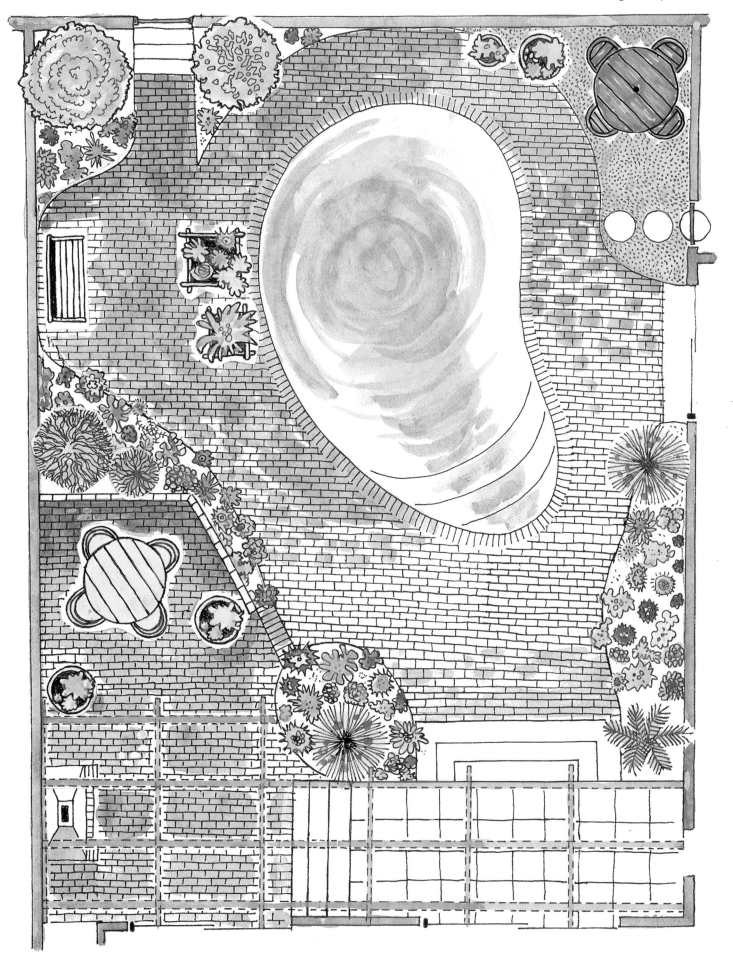

3. DRAINAGE

No building project should be started until you are quite sure that rainwater will be led away neatly to the nearest drainage channel. If you fail to do this, your lovely patio will become a standing pool in wet weather and your lawn a swamp. This is why every smooth surface, like a patio, a concrete slab or even a garden path must be laid with a slight slope in the direction in which you want the water to flow.

A descent of 1 in for every six feet is fine for patios. One side of a pathway should be ½ in lower than the other to allow for proper drainage.

For garden projects you can simply use a spirit level to determine these slopes, by taking 'skew readings'. To do this, you have the air bubble not quite centred between the two lines and just touching one of them. If, for example, you want the surface to slope towards the right, you have the bubble touching the line on the left side.

A warning: When using this method to determine the fall, it often appears that the slope is too small. It is tempting to decide to move the bubble just a little further, so it actually crosses the line. Don't. The edge of the bubble should just barely touch the line. In nature, a drop of only a hundredth of an inch is enough to drain water away. If your slope is too steep, your furrows are likely to soon become canyons.

When you have to lay drainage channels, pipes and so on over a long distance, there is an even easier technique to determine the correct slope: give your straight-edge a 'built-in' fall by nailing a small block to the underside of one end. Always place this block on the peg that determines the lower side of the slope, then take your reading 'level' in the normal way – in other words get the bubble positioned exactly in the centre between the two lines.

You can calculate the thickness of the block. It will vary according to the length of your straight-edge. A drop of 1 in for every ten feet is suitable for most construction projects.

Drainage channels

To ensure good drainage for an outdoor project like a patio usually means that you will have to build a drainage channel somewhere. The easiest is simply a semi-circular sectioned concrete channel. The technique for ensuring an even slope throughout its length is the same as for any other project where good drainage is important.

The secret is to hammer in plenty of pegs, each one just a trifle higher (or lower) than the previous one. Do it as follows:

☐ Hammer a peg in at the lowest point. (You can make your own wooden pegs, but pieces of reinforcing rod work much better, particularly in stony ground.)
☐ The lowest point is usually the gully at the end of one of your gutter downpipes.
☐ Place the block on the underside of

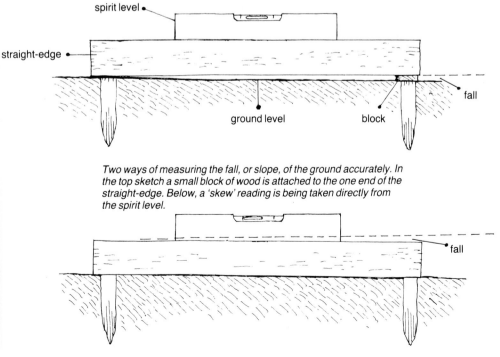

Two ways of measuring the fall, or slope, of the ground accurately. In the top sketch a small block of wood is attached to the one end of the straight-edge. Below, a 'skew' reading is being taken directly from the spirit level.

your straight-edge on the peg you hammered in at the lowest point, determine the position of the next peg, and hammer it in. Place your spirit level on the straight-edge and tap the second peg in until the bubble indicates an exact level. Place the straight-edge and spirit level on the second peg and repeat the whole process.

□ Scrape the ground with the straight-edge until the top of each peg is exactly level with the surface. Tamp the ground down firmly and add soil if necessary.

□ Now lay the various segments of the concrete channel on top of the pegs. All that remains is to pour a little mortar here and there to hold the channel steady, and to cement the joints between the sections with mortar.

Hint
When you need to take a whole series of readings over distances wider than your spirit level, you can save time by taping the spirit level to the straight-edge with masking tape.

Patios
Determine the direction of the slope of your patio so that the water will run down to the nearest drainage channel. Obviously, no part of the patio can be lower than this drainage point.

Find the vapor barrier in the wall of your house. The vapor barrier is a strip of waterproof material set between two courses of bricks and positioned a course or two above ground level. It prevents

moisture rising into the porous wall and causing damp problems.

If you plan to lay the bricks of your patio right against the wall of your house, they must not be higher than the vapor barrier. The same applies to any footpath or concrete slab you wish to lay against the side wall of your house. In practice any surface should be laid at least two brick courses below the vapor barrier.

The reason for this is simple: if the bricks or concrete are above the vapor barrier, they form a bridge across which dampness from the soil or rainwater can penetrate the wall of your house. Within six months you will pay the price – the inside and outside of the wall will begin to go mouldy and the paint will peel.

Measuring with your hose
You can also use the garden hose to determine the heights of the pegs. It may sound crazy, but it is based on the principle that water finds its own level, and it works well. This is how it is done:

□ Fit two pieces of transparent plastic tubing into the two ends of your garden hose. Now hold the two pipes together and draw or file two lines opposite each other at the same height on the transparent tubing.

□ Now hammer in long pegs, pipes or treated poles at all the places where you want to measure the highest or lowest points of your slope. The pegs must stick up at least 3 feet above ground level.

□ Fill your hose with water, hold one end against any one of the pegs and stick it

there with adhesive tape or masking tape. Draw a mark on the peg opposite the mark you made on the clear pipe.

□ Now hold the free end of the hose at about the same height against each of the other pegs. Raise or lower the hose until the water level is opposite the mark you made on the first peg, then mark the peg opposite the water level in the free end of the hose. In this way you can ensure that all the marks on your pegs are at the same level.

□ Now, by measuring an equal distance down each peg, from the mark, you can obtain a level at the foot of the peg. If, for example, you want one point to be 1 in lower than another, you simply add 1 in to your measurement and mark the peg at that point.

□ Now stretch a line tightly between each of the lower marks and knock in little pegs along this line, so their tops are at the same height as the line.

□ Now remove the line and smooth the earth level with the peg tops. Your ground will then have the correct slope.

Hint
Overfill the hose slightly at first, so you can get rid of any unwanted bubbles in it. Make sure you do not lose any water from the hose while you are taking measurements, and cork up the tube ends as you transport the hose around the site.

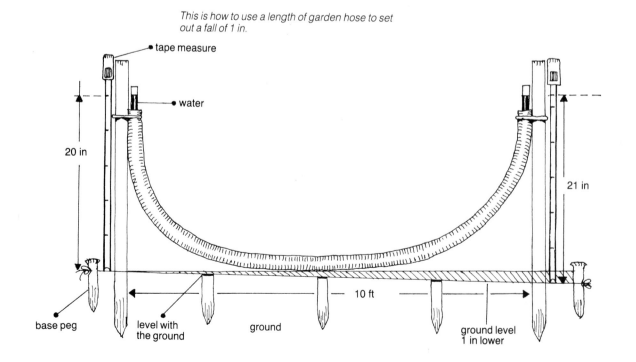

This is how to use a length of garden hose to set out a fall of 1 in.

tape measure

water

20 in

21 in

base peg

level with the ground

ground

10 ft

ground level 1 in lower

4. MORTAR

One of the first jobs you must learn to do if you want to be a bricklayer, is to mix mortar. It is not difficult and takes a short while, particularly as only small batches are usually mixed at a time.

Various mixtures can be used, your choice depending on the particular application. In all cases the ingredients must be measured out as accurately as possible, using a bucket as a measure.

The following mixtures are recommended:

mixture	cement	builder's lime	sand
1.	1	0.50	4
2.	1	1	5

*Use Portland cement with approval of American Society for Testing Materials (ASTM) on the bag.

Uses
Mixture 1: retaining walls, outside walls below the vapor barrier, face bricks, underground work, window sills, free-standing outdoor walls.
Mixture 2: outside walls, above and below the vapor barrier, inner walls, chimneys, plastered brickwork, free-standing outdoor walls.

Use a builder's bucket or an old paint bucket with a sturdy handle for measuring out quantities.

Builder's lime
It is always good practice to use builder's lime in your mortar mixture. It makes the mortar far more workable and increases the binding and water retention properties of the mixture, particularly if the sand is rather coarse. It also helps to prevent cracks in the final product. Always use hydrated builder's lime, which is available from supply stores in 50 lb sacks. Agricultural and other types of lime are not suitable. Special plasticizers can also be obtained from supply stores, and can be substituted for lime in the proportions recommended by the additive manufacturer. They have the advantage of being easier than lime to store without deteriorating.

Mixing technique
First place the sand on a clean, hard surface, such as a concrete slab. Make a hollow in the middle of the pile by sticking your spade in and drawing it towards the sides.

Pour the builder's lime and cement into the crater you have made and flatten it with a jabbing motion of the spade. Now slide the spade under the side of the heap and pour the mixture onto the centre to

form a pyramid shape. Move around the heap doing this, then flatten it again with your spade. Repeat this until the mixture has a uniformly grey colour.

Now make another crater and pour in some of the water – rather too little than too much. Form another pyramid as you move around the heap and then flatten it again with your spade.

Make another crater and add a bit more water. Repeat the process. Be particularly careful when you add the last of the water, because mortar has a nasty habit of suddenly becoming too sloppy.

Test the mixture by sticking the spade into the mixture from above and drawing it towards you with an up-and-down action. If the corrugations made in this way are so sloppy that they simply flatten out, you have added too much water. You will have to add more of the dry ingredients in the correct proportions, and mix them in well.

If the ridges look dry and crumbly, you should add a little more water. The mixture is ready when the ridges stay sharp and firm. Another test is to take a handful of mortar and squeeze it. If it retains the shape of your hand without flowing away or crumbling, it is the correct consistency.

Always remember the basic rule that applies to concrete and mortar: Add only enough water to bind the components together. Too much or too little water weakens the mixture and makes it difficult to work with.

1

2

3

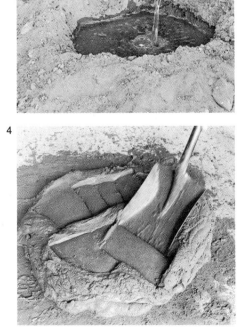

4

1. Mix the dry sand, cement and building lime or plasticizer thoroughly until the mixture is an even grey colour.
2. Form a crater and pour in part of the water – take care not to pour too much!
3. Mix from the edges toward the centre, building a pyramid. Flatten it, then repeat the process.
4. Test the mixture by jabbing the spade up and down in it while drawing the spade toward you.

5. LAYING FOUNDATIONS

If you want to erect a garden wall, barbecue, terrace wall, planter or any other structure in your garden, you need a good foundation for the brickwork. And a good foundation does not simply mean one that is strong enough to carry the weight of the wall. It must be exactly even and level, regardless of the slope of the ground, and it should not spoil the good looks of the wall by sticking up above the level of the ground.

Two kinds of foundation are important for the do-it-yourselfer who wants to do building work in his garden: strip foundations and stepped strip foundations.

Strip foundations

A strip foundation is used on level ground, and is the simplest foundation of all. It should be a minimum of 6 in thick and twice as wide as the masonry bearing on it (three times as wide for structures over 3 feet high). Foundations must be laid below the frost line.

To ensure that the trench is dug straight, hammer in pegs at each end and stretch builder's line between them, to indicate the foundation width.

The floor of the trench should be as even as possible and the sides vertical.

Use the following method to ensure that the surface of the foundation will be level:
☐ Hammer a square wooden peg or a length of reinforcing rod into the ground at the lowest point of the trench to within about 6 in below the top of the trench. Hammer the next peg about 3 feet from it into the floor of the trench and use a spirit level to ensure that the tops of both pegs are at the same height. The distance between the pegs is determined by the length of your spirit level. If your spirit level is very short, place it on a straight-edge or plank. Repeat the process until you reach the end of the trench.
☐ Now remove any surplus earth between the pegs to ensure that the concrete can be poured to the same thickness from one end of the foundation to the other.

☐ Now wet the trench well with a hose and pour in the concrete level with the top of each peg. Prod the concrete with a pole or a rigid piece of iron to get rid of any air bubbles. Scrape and tamp the surface until smooth using the side of a stout straight-edge.
☐ Wait for 24 hours before you begin to build, and simply leave the pegs embedded in the concrete.

Hint
Each time you use the spirit level to determine the height of the next peg, turn it around so the alternate end faces forward. This will reduce the likelihood of obtaining an inaccurate reading, and will compensate for a possibly faulty spirit level or straight-edge.

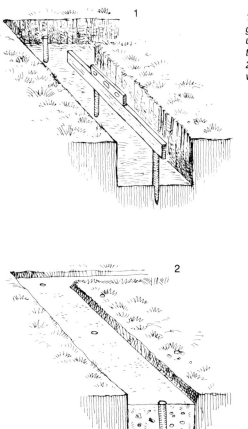

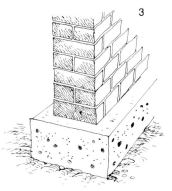

1. This is how a strip foundation is made for a garden wall. Hammer pegs into the trench and use a spirit level and straight-edge to get their tops exactly level.
2. Pour the concrete level with the peg tops; when it has set, build your wall on it.

The photograph on the left shows how a single wall, built on a simple strip foundation, can be very pleasing to the eye.

A garden wall on a stepped foundation. Note that the height of a step is equal to the height of one (or more) brick course. Also note that in this case the foundation has been made too high. It should be at least 6 in below the level of the ground.
Photograph right: This retaining wall follows the slope of the garden in steps.

Stepped strip foundations

When your ground slopes, you will find you eventually have to dig deeper and deeper to keep the floor of the trench level. This involves a whole lot more work and you will waste a good deal of concrete, mortar and bricks before your wall eventually rises above ground level. The solution is to create steps in the foundation, so it rises with the slope of the ground.

The big secret is that each step must be exactly the height of one or more bricks plus the thickness of the mortar layers.

This is how to go about it:

☐ As already mentioned, the concrete must be at least 6 in thick. Hammer the first peg in at the lowest point of the trench so its top is 6 in above the floor of the trench. Now hammer the next peg in about 6 feet from the first and use your spirit level to get the tops exactly level.

☐ Carry on like this until only about 4 in, or two thirds, of the next peg sticks out above trench bottom. This is where you make your first step. If the step is to be just one brick high, make it as follows:

☐ Hammer in a second peg alongside this one so its point is 2¾ in (the height of a single brick plus a layer of mortar) higher. Now hammer in the next lot of pegs level with the new height, until it becomes necessary to make another step.

☐ When all the pegs are in, remove the surplus earth between them so each peg sticks up 6 in (the thickness of the concrete) above the trench bottom.

☐ At each step you can pack a row of bricks across the trench to hold the concrete in place. All that remains is for you to pour the concrete level with the top of each peg.

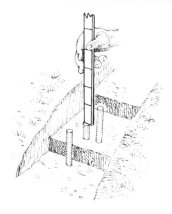

About two-thirds of the first peg should stick up above the ground. To make the step, a second peg is knocked in until it is exactly level with the first. Place your measuring stick on this second peg and knock in a third peg until it is exactly one brick course (brick plus mortar) higher than the second one.

Now dig the trench deeper until each peg sticks out 6 in (the depth of the concrete) above the bottom of the trench.

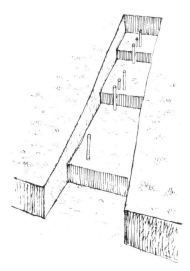

Pour the concrete level with the peg tops, and simply leave the pegs buried in the concrete.

This is what a stepped foundation looks like when it is completed. It follows the slope of the ground in steps and saves you a considerable amount of spadework, concrete and bricks.

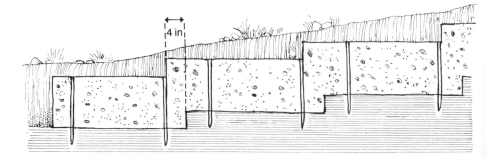

6. EDGINGS

Sturdy edgings are extremely important when you do brickwork in the garden or lay a patio or pathway. Without them, your bricks will sooner or later begin to loosen around the edges, and grass will start to encroach. (The various edgings that can be used for concrete slabs, and the shuttering method, in particular, are discussed on page 72.) Retaining walls, which are based on the same principles, are important in that they allow you to create various levels in your garden.

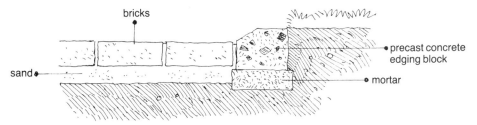

Edging bricks that have been laid on their ends on a bed of mortar.

Left: Proper edging is essential if you want your patio paving bricks to stay in position for a lifetime.

Concrete edging

Three edging methods are shown below.
1. Use of precast concrete edging blocks. These must be laid accurately square on a layer of mortar about 1½ in thick. Use a mixture of one part cement to five parts building sand.

Mark the outline of the perimeter blocks before digging the foundation, to determine how the pavers will fit, and to avoid unnecessary cutting. Use a builder's line to ensure that the edging is laid straight, and remember to allow for drainage holes and the correct slope.

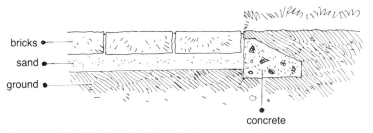

A precast concrete edging block that has been laid on a bed of mortar.

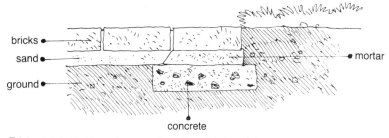

Concrete edging block cast in place after the bricks have been laid.

Edging bricks that have been mortared to a strip foundation.

2. You can also cast your own edging blocks. Make the shuttering and use a standard concrete mixture (see page 68 for details).

The concrete can be made level with the bricks which means, of course, that it will be visible. Alternatively, it can be concealed by dropping it below the surface by the depth of half a brick. Slope the concrete at an angle, however, to allow for topsoil of a sufficient depth to support grass.

3. A trench-foundation can be made (see page 25), so that the bricks around the edges can be laid on a layer of mortar. Again, use a standard concrete mixture and lay the edging bricks first.

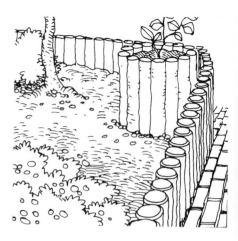

Dry-packed stones can make an effective retaining edging.

Bricks

Bricks can be stood on their ends to form an edging. First, make shuttering to hold the bricks in a straight line. Pack the bricks firmly against the inside of the shuttering. Throw a channel of mortar along the bottom of your trench, to hold the bricks lightly in position. Wait until the mortar is dry, then remove the shuttering. Throw another strip of mortar along the outside of the bricks.

If the ground is firm enough, the sides of the trench can be made vertical and the bricks laid in position without the use of shuttering or mortar.

Wooden poles

Short wooden poles sunk into the ground can make an attractive edging for footpaths, patios and flower beds. They make excellent retaining walls, too, as shown in the sketches and photographs.

Retaining walls made of treated logs are not only sturdy, but have a lovely natural appearance, particularly when combined with plants.

In the sketches on this page you can see how a retaining wall can be built by laying logs crisscrossed on top of each other. Secure the logs by drilling holes through their ends and bolting them together. There are proprietary fixings known in the trade as log clamps which are worth using if they are available.

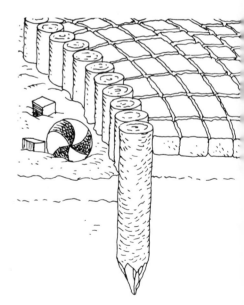

Above: Short, wooden logs can be used as an edging which is both practical and attractive.

Left and right: Thick wooden poles serve as effective edging.

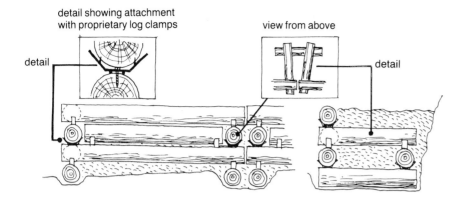

detail showing attachment
with proprietary log clamps

view from above

detail

detail

*Left: Treated logs held firmly in position can
form an ideal retaining wall.*

7. GARDEN WALLS

Building a wall in your garden is not as complicated as you might expect. The following is a 'practice project', which can be used to build a garden wall, retaining wall or planter, as it will teach you the basic principles of brickwork. Once you can keep the wall and its corners straight, you will be well on the way to becoming a bricklayer.

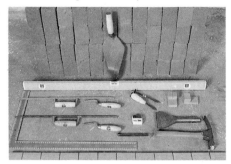

1. Your first job is to make yourself a simple gauge rod (front; see page 38 for instructions). This photograph shows the other basic equipment you will need for building a wall: a mason's trowel, spirit level, builder's set-square (instructions for a home-made set-square are given on page 37), pointing tools (long, short, square or round, depending on the sort of pointing joint you select), builder's line with pegs, corner blocks (instructions on page 38), chisel (for cutting bricks) and hammer, measuring tape and a joint scraper (DIY from sheet metal).

2. Roll builder's line the length of your wall around two bricks and stretch the line taut.

If you use the practice project described in this chapter, you can easily achieve a professional result.

3. Mark out the corner of the wall, using a square. In this way you can be certain that the corners of the wall will be at right angles.

4. Mark out the length of the wall. (When you do this in the actual garden, you will be working on top of your foundation.)

5. Now lay your bricks along the building line to see how they will fit. Use your gauge rod or a pointing tool to space

the bricks, and shift the corner until you can get only whole bricks to fit in.

Pack a neat pile of bricks next to your corner and see that all your tools are close at hand before you begin to mix the mortar. See page 23 for the appropriate mixture to use and how to mix it.

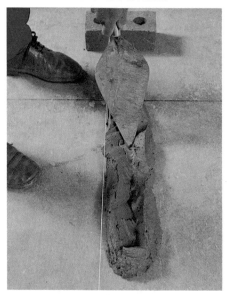

6. Pour enough mortar for two bricks onto the foundation alongside the line and use the trowel point, with a tapping action, to scrape a little furrow in the centre of the mortar. Now lay the corner brick and tap it with the edge of the trowel until it is level with your builder's line. Do not let the brick touch the line – always keep it just away from the line to prevent its throwing the string out of true.

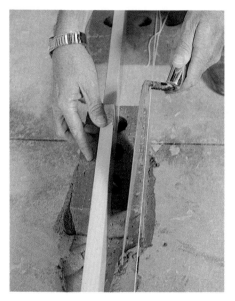

7. Test whether the brick is lying level by placing your spirit level on it lengthways and crossways. The air bubble should always be exactly centred.

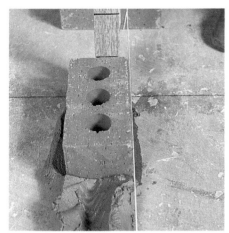

8. Also test the height of the brick by standing your gauge rod against it vertically. The first mark on your measuring stick should be level with the top of the brick.

9. Now 'butter' the end of the second brick with mortar and lay it against the corner brick. Test again with the spirit level in both directions to ensure that both are the same height and level. If not, lift the second brick and add a little mortar.

10. Lay a row of three bricks in this way before you begin building the other angle.

11. Check the corner again with your square to make doubly sure that it forms a right angle. Tap any skew brick into place, using the trowel's edge.

12. Throw cement on the two corner bricks and lay the first brick of the second course.

13. Tap the brick with the edge of the trowel until it is lying correctly, then use the gauge rod to ensure that it is the correct height. Scrape off excess mortar by sweeping the trowel forward and upward against the brick. Do not do shoddy work here. You are building the

corner without the benefit of a building line, so every brick must be laid level and at the correct height; if your corners are out, all the bricks you lay between the corners will be out of alignment, too.

14. Once the corner begins to take shape, check regularly by laying the spirit level diagonally against the outside surface to ensure that there are no bulges or hollows.

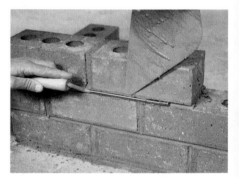

15. Smooth the joints with your pointing tool. At the same time, draw the trowel point along the top of the brick to clean off excess mortar.

16. This completes one corner. Now build the other corner: use corner blocks to stretch the building line between the two, and lay the bricks along it. Because you do not need to use the spirit level so often, progress is faster.

Single walls

Single brick walls are usually built in gardens, but if they are on the longish side, they must be supported at least every 6 feet by a built-in pier or buttress. If the wall is completely free-standing, you must have a vertical expansion joint for the whole height of the wall every 25 feet.

The accompanying sketches show how this is done. The sketches also show how the bricks on alternate courses (layers) are laid on top of each other, and where bricks should be cut.

Two methods of building a pillar are also shown.

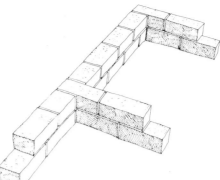

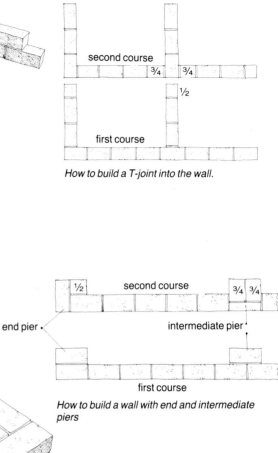

How to build a T-joint into the wall.

How to build a wall with end and intermediate piers

Outer corner with single stretcher bond

Two methods of building pillars

Garden wall with reinforced attached pier

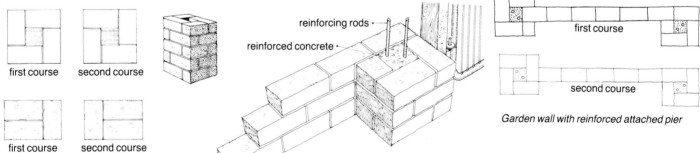

Use corner blocks and a tingle to hold the builder's line in position. On page 38 we show you how to make a measuring stick (or gauge) and corner block. Cut the tingle from a piece of sheet metal.

Building with profiles

Once you start pottering around your home with trowel and cement, you will find that a number of handy tricks of the builder's trade will make your tasks a lot easier.

On page 34, you were shown how to build a single wall by first erecting the corners and then the rest of the wall, using corner blocks to stretch the line between the corners. This method is the traditional one, and it works well. However, it does take a bit of time and patience, because the position of every corner brick must be checked and rechecked for accuracy with a spirit level before the next one can be laid.

The sooner you get your builder's lines stretched at the correct height, the sooner – and more easily – you can lay the bricks. The problem arises when you have no corner on which to base your line. How do you overcome this?

First method
Buy yourself two pieces of square tubing about 6 feet long, known in building terms as 'hollow profiles'.

Stand one of these profiles up at one end of the wall, ensuring that one of its sides is more-or-less plumb with the planned brick face. Hammer nails at an angle through the ends of two longish planks, turn the planks over and hook their nails into the top of the square tubing to form a sturdy pyramid, then secure the base of each plank with a couple of bricks.

Now hold your spirit level firmly against the profile and shift the support planks until the front and the side surfaces of the profile are exactly vertical. Repeat the process at the point where the other 'corner' of the wall is to be built.

Now hold your gauge rod up against the profile and mark out the heights of the various brick courses (layers). Your 'corners' are ready. All you have to do now is hook the corner blocks around the profiles at the correct height, with the tightly-stretched line between them. When one row of bricks has been laid, simply move the corner blocks up to the next mark.

Use your spirit level from time to time to check that your two profiles are still vertical. If they have been knocked out of position without your realising it, your whole wall will be crooked.

Above right: This is how a corner profile made of square tubing is set up. Note how the bottom of the support plank is held in position with bricks.
Right: the gauge rod is used to mark the position of the brick courses on the profile.

Set-square method

An even quicker and cheaper method is to make yourself two large set-squares of wood for use as corner profiles. They can also be used to ensure that the corners of your patios and concrete slabs are exactly square. Use 1 x 2 planks and select ones that are perfectly straight.

So that the set-square can double as a measuring stick, draw lines about 2¾ in apart (the thickness of a brick plus a layer of mortar) on one arm. Assemble the set-square as shown in the accompanying sketch and finish it off with a couple of coats of varnish. This will ensure that it will not warp when it gets wet.

Test the accuracy of your set-square by drawing a straight line on a smooth concrete surface, or making a straight line on the floor with a chalk line. Using your set-square, draw a 90° angle on this line. Now turn the set-square around and draw another 90° angle alongside the first. The two lines should be exactly parallel.

You can also test them by placing the two set-squares back-to-back on a flat surface. The two vertical sides should fit together perfectly.

Place the set-square on its side at the point where the corner of your wall is to

be, and anchor one of its 'feet' by packing a few bricks on it. Hammer a nail at an angle through a roofing slat or any other piece of plank, and hook the nail over the top of the triangle.

Check with your spirit level until the set-square is standing exactly vertical, then anchor the foot of the support plank firmly with bricks. Check once again to ensure that nothing has moved.

Place the second set-square in position where the other corner is to come. Repeat the whole procedure. Once both set-squares have been set up, all you have to do is stretch your builder's line between them, with the help of your corner blocks.

Hint

The builder's line is always stretched along the outside of a wall and you should always work from that side. All your building material must be set out on the outside, too. And remember the golden rule: no brick should ever actually touch the line – there should always be a tiny space between the brick's edge and the line, to prevent the line being forced out of true, which would result in a crooked wall.

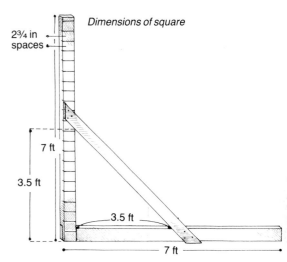

Dimensions of square

2¾ in spaces

7 ft

3.5 ft

3.5 ft

7 ft

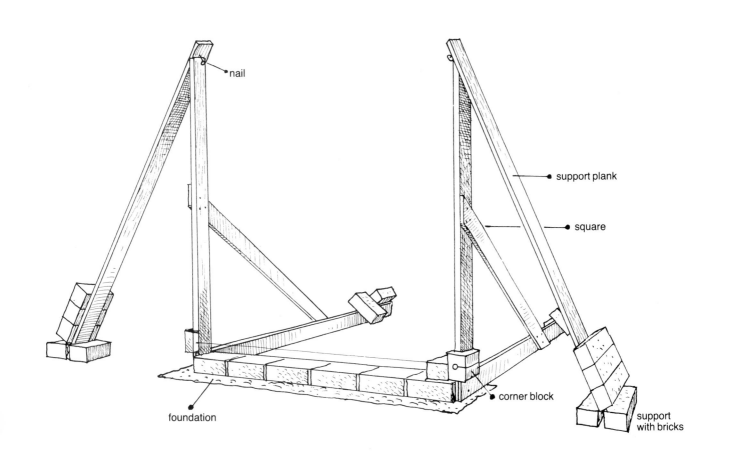

nail

support plank

square

corner block

foundation

support with bricks

Home-made squares are used here as profiles. The sketch, above right, gives the dimensions of the square.

Making your own corner blocks

You will not be able to buy corner blocks anywhere – you have to make them yourself.
Use roofing battens (measuring 1½ x 1½ in) or any other suitable wood, as shown.

1. Saw the piece of roofing batten or other wood as shown in the photograph.

3. Wrap the builder's line around the block and pass it through the slot again.

2. Saw a notch in the blocks and pass the end of the builder's line through the slot.

4. Wrap the builder's line around the other side of the block.

5. Pass it through the slot again. Now hook the block around a corner brick or profile, stretch the string very tightly and hook the other block around the opposite corner.

Making a gauge rod

You will have to make this, too. Use 2 x 2s about six feet long and, with the help of a set-square, draw a series of lines about 2¾ in apart along its edge. (This measurement is the average depth of a brick plus a roughly ½ in layer of mortar.)

Because the thickness of bricks can vary, it is best to work out for yourself just how far apart the lines on your measuring stick should be. To do this, simply pack five or six bricks against each other and measure their total thickness; divide this figure by the number of bricks to get an average. Add to this the thickness of a layer of mortar.

How to lay bricks

Separate a pear-shaped lump of mortar

Scoop it onto the trowel

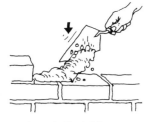

Drop the mortar onto the bricks

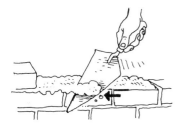

Scrape off the surplus mortar

Scrape a groove in the mortar

Butter the end of the next brick

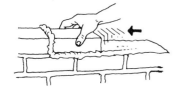

Slide the brick into position

Good brickwork is a bricklayer's pride and joy and a pleasure to look at.

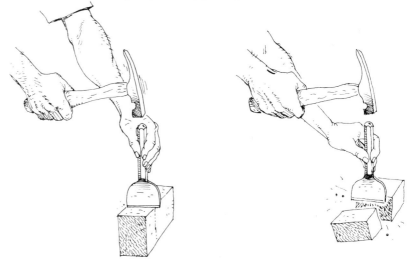

The right way to cut a brick
Place the brick on the ground and position the chisel on the cutting line. Hit the chisel just hard enough to make a mark on the brick. Turn the brick on its side and repeat the procedure. Now place the brick with its underside up and position the chisel on the cutting line again. Give the chisel a good, hard blow. The brick should break all along the cutting lines.

Building an archway

An archway in a brick wall tends to look aesthetically more pleasing than a squared-off opening or simply a gap.

The first step is to make a semi-circle of wood to support the bricks while the mortar is setting. This structure is known as a 'turning piece' or 'former'. This is how you make a former.

Lay a piece of chipboard flat on the ground and mark out your semi-circle with a pencil attached to a piece of string fixed to a central point; its length is based on the following simple formula: the height (radius) of the arch equals half the width of the opening.

Saw out the curve and use it as a pattern to make another semi-circle the same shape and size. Cut this out and attach the two semi-circles together with little wooden blocks, ensuring that the depth of the finished former matches that of your wall. Now give the little blocks a continuous surface by nailing a strip of hardboard over them. Use your measuring stick to mark out the positions of the bricks around the circumference of the former. If you cannot get whole bricks to fit in perfectly, you will have to increase or decrease the width of the mortar joints between them until they do fit.

Now build up the wall until it reaches arch height. Support the turning piece on vertical beams, each of which rests on two overlapping wedges. Tap the wedges with a hammer until the turning piece is level and at the correct height.

Place your keystone temporarily in position on the centre of the turning piece and then use your gauge rod to ensure that this brick will be in line with the first course of bricks to be built over the arch.

Lay the first two bricks on either side of the turning piece, to prevent it from shifting around, then continue upwards, keeping to the markings on your former; lay the keystone last. Now complete the rest of the wall, course by course, building each layer of bricks up to the arch.

Leave the former in position for at least three days to allow the mortar to set properly. Remove it by tapping out the wedges under the supporting beams.

A facebrick archway adds a graceful touch unmatched by an ordinary gateway.

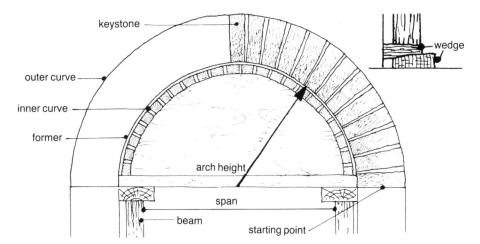

This is how the former (also called a turning piece) is set up to build an arch. The inset shows how the support beams are positioned – use a pair of wedges that slide over each other to adjust the height.

An arch can be built up in two ways: with a timber former or with an old tire (at ground level only).

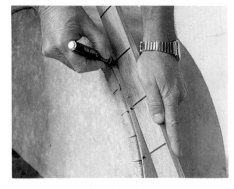

1. Mark the position of the bricks on the former using your gauge rod.

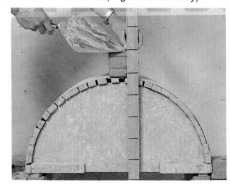

2. Make sure your keystone will be in line with the first unbroken course of bricks that will be laid over the top of the arch.

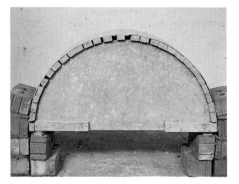

3. Hold the former in position by supporting it on bricks or props.

4. The keystone (key brick) is the last to be mortared in position.

8. WAYS WITH WALLS

There is no reason why the boundary walls of your property should look like long, boring, prison walls. As you can see from our photographs, there are plenty of ways to avoid monotony.

A wall built of sturdy wooden poles is striking; a similar effect can be obtained by placing the poles between brick pillars.

The monotony of a high, street-facing wall can be broken by creating slits in it at regular intervals. Make the slits 4 in wide, separated by 4 in of wall (see sketch).

A plant container that forms part of the wall is not an expensive addition, and it can transform the whole appearance of a wall. A high wall that drops to the level of the entrance gate in a graceful curve gives a far more harmonious effect than one which ends abruptly and towers over the gate.

Remember that you will have to build walls just inside your property boundary, since the wall foundations must not extend outside it. Contact your local planning or building board for advice on height or boundary requirements.

Remember that walls should incorporate piers every 6 feet, and that there should also be an expansion joint every 15 feet.

Left: A slight curve rounds off this high wall.
Right, above: Neat stonework is hard to beat as a front wall.
Right: Stone, poles and bricks used in combination.

9. STEPS

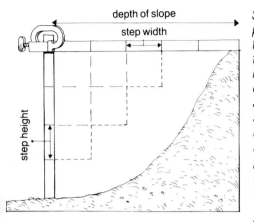

Set up a profile where you want to build steps. This will allow you to work out the number of steps and the height and width of each one accurately.

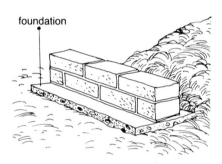

Lay a foundation and build a low wall.

Lay concrete to support the bricks and pavers.

Build the next wall and repeat the whole process until you reach the top of the slope.

Somewhere in your garden, you are probably going to need a step or two – and most people are frightened off this project by the measuring work necessary to ensure that the steps fit the slope and that each step is exactly the same height and width. Actually, it is not difficult at all. All you need to make the measuring simple is a profile consisting of two planks to indicate the highest and lowest levels and the depth of the slope.

The ideal height of every step is about 7 in and the width, measured from front to back, 10 in, but in a garden you can adapt these freely to suit your materials and the plan of the garden. The above measurements are given simply as guidelines.

Use your spirit level to get the horizontal plank of your profile level, and then mark out the number of steps on the vertical plank. Divide the length of the slope by the number of steps you want, to find the width of each step. Mark out these widths along your horizontal plank.

Now hold your spirit level vertically against each of these marks to transfer the widths of the steps to the ground.

Use the following method to make steps of brick, concrete paving blocks or crazy paving.

Pour a light concrete foundation where you want the first (bottom) step to come, and on it build a 'wall' comprising two courses of bricks. Remove some of the earth behind the bricks, fill up the gap with concrete which extends into a 'platform' about one brick deep to support the paving blocks or bricks (see sketch).

Along the back edge of the paving blocks lay a course of bricks for the next step. Repeat this process until you reach the top. The flight of steps can, of course, be built entirely of bricks, as illustrated.

Top: Stone slabs laid at regular intervals are an easy way to build steps, particularly in an informal garden.
Above: Another easy way to build steps: old timbers with concrete between them. Drill holes through the timbers and hammer reinforcing rods through to hold them in position.

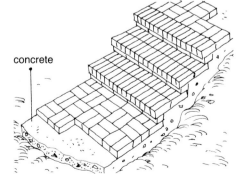

A brick pathway and steps laid on concrete instead of on firmly-tamped earth.

10. BUILD A PRACTICAL BARBECUE

Trying to provide plans for the perfect barbecue is about as difficult as providing the instructions for grilling a perfect medium-rare steak or making up the ideal chili sauce.

This is because everyone has his own favourite recipe, his own method of cooking, favourite barbecue fuel or his own, personal way of controlling the height of the grid or grill.

One school of thought believes in scorching the meat an inch or so above the coals, the steak-house way – as though it were always well-aged steak. In the process, they keep turning the grid and sprinkling cup after cup of wine, or water, on the coals to prevent the flames turning the meat to charcoal.

The other school believes that no grid should ever be very close to the coals. You do not scorch a chop or a sausage like you do a steak, they argue: you gently nurse it to perfection in the best spice of all – the smoke that rises from the glowing coals below.

Left: This circular barbecue allows the chef and his guests to enjoy the open fire together or to gather round a cooking pot. It's the ideal project for the do-it-yourself bricklayer, and plans for building it are given on pages 48-49.
Below: All the fire-making materials are close at hand if you build this storage space into your barbecue.

An open barbecue with space for two grids – or a pot simmering gently to one side. It also offers alternative working positions, according to the wind direction.

With such strong preferences apparent, it is not surprising that there are patents on much of today's barbecue equipment: grids; devices for regulating the height of the grid and for preventing the meat from falling off the grid; special meat tongs and forks; and chimneys that, it is claimed, will prevent smoke from getting into your eyes and clothing. And each designer insists that his innovation is the greatest.

Somewhere amidst all the patents and paraphernalia, something very important has been lost: the simple pleasure of gathering around an open fire.

These days it is regarded as most unseemly by some 'experts' to build a barbecue without a chimney. Such a barbecue is often built against a wall, because that is the only way it can be fitted in, and many of them suffer from the same fault – they do not draw well. All of them come with a double guarantee: that the host will have to stand with his back to his guests while he cooks the meat, and that nobody else will see a single glowing coal through all the smoke. The whole affair, with its senseless chimney, costs a fortune, and there is seldom a decent place to sit or put down your wine glass. Yet everybody builds one because the Joneses next door have one.

Section A – A

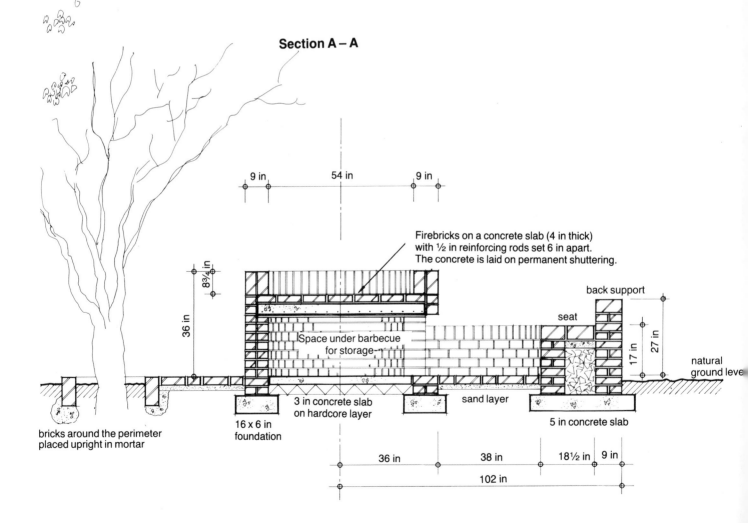

9 in   54 in   9 in

Firebricks on a concrete slab (4 in thick) with ½ in reinforcing rods set 6 in apart. The concrete is laid on permanent shuttering.

back support

seat

8¾ in

36 in

Space under barbecue for storage

17 in   27 in

natural ground level

bricks around the perimeter placed upright in mortar

16 x 6 in foundation

3 in concrete slab on hardcore layer

sand layer

5 in concrete slab

36 in   38 in   18½ in   9 in

102 in

Plan of barbecue area

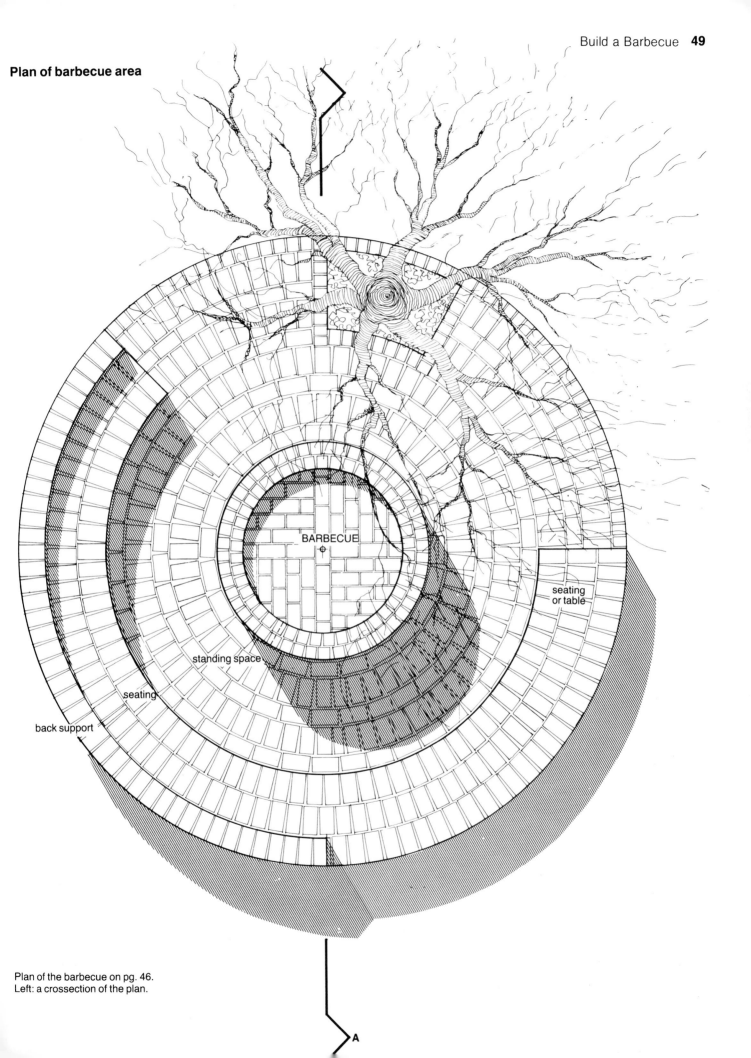

BARBECUE

seating
or table

standing space

seating

back support

Plan of the barbecue on pg. 46.
Left: a crossection of the plan.

A

With all the complicated inventions available for turning a grid, this looks too simple to be true. The peg on the underside of the grid acts as a pivot on which the grid is turned over effortlessly.
Below: With this circular barbecue, up to 25 guests can be entertained comfortably around the fire, and there is enough seating for everyone. The baking oven provides the occasional loaf of traditional bread.

The plans for circular barbecues offered here have none of the Jones's problems. There are no chimneys, and in both cases there is plenty of seating space for your guests. This same space provides a place to stand your glass or rest your plate. The meat is not cooked in a cave; everyone can stand around and see the fire – and the host does not have to stand with his back to his guests. If the smoke bothers you, you can simply move upwind of the fire. The grid height is not controlled by complicated pulleys, jacks, or any other gimmick. You can simply turn it over, without using much muscle power and without splashing grease or fat on your smart patio paving. In each case, there is enough space for two or more grids, a cooking pot, the side dishes and even a separate fire.

Both types are inexpensive and easy to build. And they both offer all-year-round garden seating, saving you the bother of having to lug chairs and tables about.

The barbecue shown on pages 46-47 is built near a tree which forms part of the barbecue area, and there is also storage space beneath for firewood. Turning the grid is simplicity itself (see photograph) and, as it is done over the fire, fat is prevented from dripping onto the surrounding paving bricks.

The grid in the barbecue shown below is supported on a simple square steel frame and the grid height is controlled by placing bricks under the feet of the frame. For those who find the idea of the steel frame a bit scary, however, there is an easy solution: leave it out. A couple of layers of bricks forming the outline of a triangle will work equally well. An advantage of using loose bricks as a grid support is that you can cook on any part of the circle, depending on the direction of the wind.

The first barbecue shown is paved with fire bricks, the second with ordinary bricks laid loose. .

The size of each of these designs can easily be adapted to suit your particular needs and available space. Extras could include the following: an electric power point that meets with outdoor specifications and lift-up seats that provide storage for foam cushions, when these are not in use.

A sketch of a rectangular barbecue, also without a chimney but with plenty of seating space, is shown right as an ideal starter. There are lots of variations possible on this sort of design.

An oblong barbecue with storage space. There is plenty of seating for everybody.
Photograph below: it is essential that a chimney draws well, unless you want to entertain your guests in a cloud of smoke. Make provision for plenty of seating space and somewhere to put down food and equipment.

11. PATIOS

An attractive patio is the focal point of your outdoor entertaining area – and it is one of the easiest outdoor construction projects you can tackle. The method discussed here is the easiest and most economical of all: bricks laid on a bed of sand. This is also a suitable method of laying a wide range of other materials like cement slabs, crazy paving and cobblestones.

The big secret of success lies in proper preparation. The ground must be thoroughly tamped down to prevent hollows and mounds forming, and sloped to ensure that rainwater will be carried away to the nearest drainage channel.

The base peg method
The first steps are to determine the direction in which the patio surface should slope and the depth to which the ground should be excavated to allow for the thickness of the paving, the layer of sand in which it is to be laid, the hardcore (clean, hard rubble, like pieces of brick, stones and coarse gravel) under the sand and the level of the vapor barrier of your house walls.

If your patio is to be right against the outer wall of your house, it must be at least the depth of one brick, or preferably two,

below the vapor barrier, to prevent moisture from being drawn into the walls.

The depth of the hardcore layer should be determined by the sort of traffic you expect over the patio. For pedestrian traffic only, it can be quite a thin layer – about 3 in deep. In fact, it is not always necessary to use hardcore. If your ground is firm or stony and not likely to subside, all you need do is remove the top layer of soil. If, however, you intend to drive a car over the paving, you should put down hardcore, or even lay a concrete slab under the bricks. (See page 72 for how to do the latter.) On top of the layer of hardcore, you will need a layer of coarse sand, about 2 in deep, on which to lay the bricks.

First, dig a trench of the required width along the wall where the patio is to be, and hammer in a base peg so that its top is at the required height of the surface of the layer of sand – in other words, to the

Left: Patio with brick planter and seat.
Below: This patio door turns the small enclosed garden into part of the living area.

base peg

1. The base peg is hammered in after a strip of ground along the wall has been excavated.

2. Now hammer in a row of pegs along the wall and use your spirit level to ensure that the top of each one is level with that of the base peg.

3. Next, knock in a second row of pegs to indicate the outline of the patio and stretch a line between these pegs. This line should indicate exactly where the outer boundary of the patio will be.

4. Use your builder's square to ensure that the corner is an exact 90° angle. Shift the pegs if the line is out. See page 83 for how to check whether all four corners are right angles.

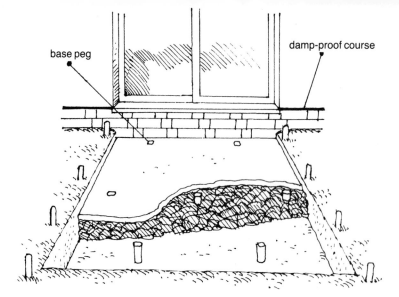

base peg

damp-proof course

damp-proof course

paving brick

hardcore

sand

base peg

ground

detail

A patio where the paving bricks have been set on a layer of sand. The detailed sketch above shows the various layers of the completed patio.

5. Remove the earth to more or less the level you have calculated, to make allowance for the hardcore, the sand, and the damp-proof course of the house wall.

6. Now hammer in more pegs, checking the level by placing one end of your straight-edge on the base peg and the other on the new peg, with your spirit level on top. Remember to drop the level of the pegs progressively in the direction in which you want the water to drain (a drop of about 1 in for every 3½ ft).

damp-proof course

7. Spread a layer of hardcore and tamp it down firmly to about 2 in below the level of the pegs.

8. Now spread a layer of sand about 2 in thick on top of the hardcore. Tamp it firm and scrape it with your straight-edge until it is smooth and level with the tops of the pegs.

Your base is now ready for the paving bricks – it is at the correct height, properly firm so the bricks will not sink, and sloped just enough to lead the rainwater away in the desired direction.

combined depth of the layer of hardcore (if you are having one) and the layer of sand on which the bricks will be laid. (Remember to allow a distance equal to at least three courses of bricks between the top of the peg and the vapor barrier – one to accommodate the layer of paving bricks or blocks, and the other two to ensure that the final surface is well below the vapor barrier.)

This means that you will have to excavate to a depth of about 12 in to make provision for between 3 and 5 in of hardcore, the layer of sand (2 in), the thickness of the paving material, and the required depth below the vapor barrier.

Alternative method
If your ground is nice and firm and you decide to lay your patio some distance from the house wall, it is not necessary to dig as deep, or to use hardcore or pegs. All you have to do is use a pick or spade to loosen the ground to a depth of about 3 in.

Rake the surface roughly level and remove all stones and weeds. Now use your straight-edge to scrape the earth level, but this time put your spirit level on the straight-edge and 'build in' the slight slope in the direction the rainwater must drain by taking uneven readings from the spirit level. This can be done by allowing the air bubble just to touch one indicator line. See page 21 for detailed instructions on how this is done.

Now tamp the earth down firmly and spread the sand on top of it. Scrape it smooth again.

Laying the bricks
Once the ground has been smoothed and firmed, you can set up building lines to mark the edge of the patio. The bricks can be laid in two ways – with or without cement joints between them.

Hint
When you are laying your first row of bricks, you usually have to kneel on the sand which you have just smoothed with such care. Work on a sheet of hardboard or a scaffolding plank to avoid making hollows in the sand. Once you have laid enough bricks, you can place the hardboard on top of them to serve as a support for your knees.

Without joints
The easiest method is to lay the bricks right against each other without any gaps between them. When you use this method, however, you must use good-quality paving bricks. Old second-hand bricks are uneven and difficult to lay straight and level.

Lay the edging bricks crossways against the side line and tap each one into position with a rubber mallet to settle it well into the sand. Then start the second row, bearing in mind that every alternate row should start with a half-brick.

Check with the spirit level regularly to ensure that the bricks are even and the correct slope is being maintained throughout. If a brick seems too low, lift it out and add sand underneath it.

When the patio is completely laid, firm, permanent edging must be added. Do not do shoddy work here. The edging actually holds the whole patio in place and the bricks around the edges will sooner or later begin to loosen if the edging gives way. Refer to Chapter 6 to see how to make a good edging.

You can, of course, lay the edging first, but then you should lay only one side before starting to lay the inside bricks. If you lay all four sides first, you will end up struggling to fit the paving bricks into place and will have to do a considerable amount of brick cutting.

Once the edging is in place, just one small task remains. Sprinkle sand down the middle of the patio and spread it around with a broom so it sifts into the gaps between the bricks. The sand wedges the bricks firmly together.

With joints
If you prefer to have a mortar join between the bricks, every brick must be precisely positioned and a builder's line used on every row. This is necessary because crooked joints will spoil the whole appearance of your patio.

The joints should be about ½ in wide and a reinforcing rod or block of wood of the correct thickness can be used to space the bricks accurately.

While wooden pegs and a line can be used to position the outside row of bricks, it is not practical to knock in a set of pegs for every row. Simply wind the line around a brick at each end, carefully position the bricks opposite each other, and stretch the line taut, to act as a guideline. If it is a particularly long row and you have difficulty keeping the line properly taut, you can support it at one or two points towards the middle – simply with folded pieces of paper, which will raise the line to the correct height (see photograph).

When all the bricks are down, the permanent edging should be laid as already described. Now fill the gaps between the bricks with mortar.
There are two ways of doing this.

In most cases it is not necessary to lay a patio on hardcore as shown on page 54. If the ground is firm enough, you can simply loosen it with a pick, then scrape it level with a straight-edge, as shown here. Use your spirit level to ensure that the ground slopes in the right direction for drainage, and tamp it down firmly before you begin laying the patio bricks.

First method

This is recommended for rather porous bricks, which would easily be stained by wet mortar.

Mix thoroughly three parts sand with one part cement and pour the dry mixture on top of the bricks. Now allow this mixture to fill the joints by sweeping it over the surface with a broom. Fit a sprinkler head to your garden hose and wet the whole patio. The water will run into the joints and cause the mortar to set. Remove any surplus cement with a thick sponge.

Second method

Mix three parts sand with one of cement and enough water to make a fairly smooth mixture. Now wet the paving well and pour the mortar mixture on top of it. See that you have a helper standing by with a yard broom. While he brushes the mortar into the joints, follow behind and prod the mortar down with the edge of a trowel to work it well into the joints. Complete small areas at a time and hose the bricks clean as you go along, to prevent mortar stains.

When all the joints are filled with mortar, the bricks can be sprayed again. Do not spray directly into the joints. Use a thick sponge to remove any excess mortar. This method is recommended for very hard, dense bricks that will not be stained by the cement. The best precaution is to do a test run: lay a few bricks and spread the cement according to the above instructions. Leave them for a couple of days and then see whether you are satisfied with the result.

With joints
1. Patio paving bricks being laid to allow for mortar joints between them. Note how the builder's line is simply wound around a brick.

2. The edging bricks are laid in position.

3. The first row of bricks is laid.

4. Each brick is correctly spaced with a pointing tool.

5. Pinch the builder's line in a folded piece of paper and place a brick on it.

6. This is how it looks when complete.

7. The mortar is swept in between the bricks.

8. Spray with a hose to clean.

9. Wipe clean with a sponge.

Without joints
The simplest method of all: bricks laid right against each other without mortar joints.
Each brick is tapped into place with a rubber mallet. When you have finished, sweep sand into the gaps between the bricks.

Patterns

As you can see from the accompanying sketches, paving can be laid in a variety of interesting patterns. Always remember, though, that the more complicated patterns will probably entail a good deal of brick cutting and a bit more expertise. The pattern shown in our colour photograph is the easiest and will present the fewest problems.

To lay bricks in a circle or semi-circle, hammer a peg into the ground in the centre of the circle and attach a string to it. At the other end, tie a large nail or stick. Pull the string taut and draw a circle or semi-circle on the ground with the nail. Lay the bricks accurately along this arc. Adjust the string and repeat the process for the next row.

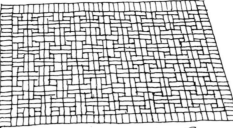

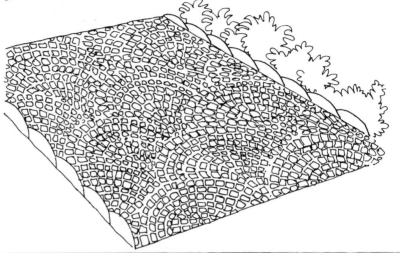

The sketches on this page show some of the many patterns and bonds in which paving can be laid. Bear in mind that more skill is required to lay complicated patterns. The pattern shown on page 56 is called stretcher bond and is the simplest of all.
Below: Cobblestone paving.

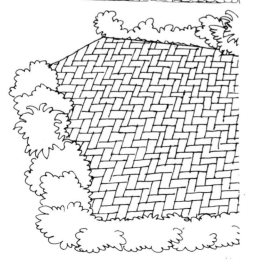

Installing a door to the patio

One of the best improvements you can make to your home is to install a door that allows you to step straight out onto your patio – preferably with its own barbecue area. This is not an expensive job.

Aluminium-framed sliding doors are, without doubt, your best bet. They do not warp, are maintenance-free and relatively easy to install once the wall-opening has been made.

You can also get aluminium doors with coloured finishes and with Georgian-style small panes or leaded lights. There are hardwood-framed doors available too.

Because installation methods differ from one manufacturer to another, and full instructions are usually enclosed with the door, we shall concentrate mainly on how to make the correct-sized opening.

Siting
Select the position of your sliding door with care, so it will form an integral part of your outdoor entertaining and relaxing area. Avoid converting an existing door or window just because it seems the easiest thing to do.

Two fixed panels, with two sliding doors in the middle, work best. If you choose a patio door with just one fixed panel and one sliding one, it is preferable not to fit it with the sliding section at right angles to an interior wall, as the wall will soon become grubby with fingerprints. You will also have the irritation of having to move the curtain out of the way every time you use the door. There is the bother, as well, of the curtain always blowing out through the open door.

When buying your door, find out from the manufacturer or supplier exactly how wide the wall-opening should be. Most sliding patio doors are fitted within a timber sub-frame which allows some slight latitude when installing the doors, but accurate measurements are essential for a trouble-free installation. It is better to choose a hardwood frame than a softwood one, which could rot in time.

Use a long, wooden straight-edge or length of square steel tubing as a ruler, and use your spirit level to get the sides of the door exactly vertical, and the top horizontal, before you begin drawing lines on the wall. It's best to actually score the face of the wall with a chisel, as its line is easily visible – even through a layer of dust.

In most cases, you will be using an existing opening – a window or a set of French doors – as the site for your new patio doors, cutting out the brickwork beneath existing sills to create the new rectangular opening for the doors. In this case the existing lintel will be left in position to bridge the opening, and no further strengthening work will be needed. However, if you want a wider opening, or you are fitting doors into an existing solid wall, a lintel will have to be fitted over the opening. Check with your local building department to see if a permit is necessary before starting work.

These full-width patio doors permit a panoramic view of garden and countryside.

1

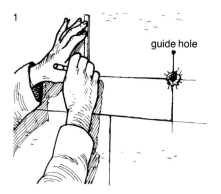

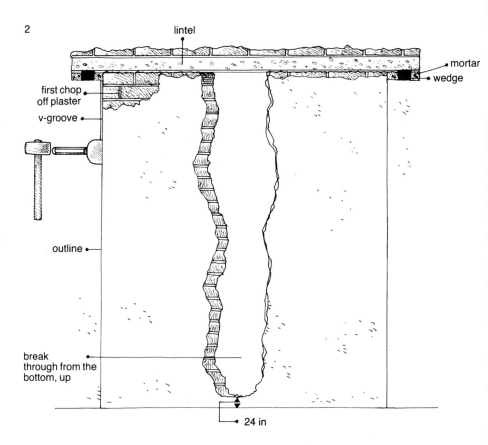

1. The position of the lintel is marked out on the inside of the wall after you have drilled two holes right through from the outside.

2. This is how to knock a hole in the wall for a sliding door. The lintel is first placed in position and held in place with wedges. Once the mortar has set, a vertical hole is knocked through the wall. The wall is then chopped away at the sides of the hole. The same method can be used to install ordinary doors and windows.

3. The edges of the opening are plastered.

First Method

When you are simply utilizing an existing window or French door opening for your patio doors, the first stage is to remove the existing window frame. To do this, unscrew the doors and opening casements and lift them aside. Then break and remove the fixed panes of glass (it's a good idea to criss-cross them with adhesive tape first to prevent pieces of broken glass from falling out all over the place). You can then saw through the frame members at each side and pry them out with a crowbar. Remove the remains of old fixing devices, and clean up all round the sides of the opening.

You can now mark the vertical cutting lines on the internal and external faces of the wall, extending downwards from the sides of the existing opening to the level of the damp proof course (dpc). The brickwork can then be chopped away with bolster and club hammer, or else cut through cleanly from each side using an angle grinder, ready to receive the new door frame.

Second Method

For new openings, or existing openings that have to be widened, a suitable lintel must be installed.

Mark where the lintel will be positioned on the outside wall, making sure it projects for the correct distance beyond each side of the opening: 6 in for lintels with a length up to 8½ feet and 12 in for lintels of 10 feet or longer.

The cutting lines must now be transferred to the inside of the wall. Drill holes right through the wall at the two points which mark the top corners of the lintel. Now go inside and draw a line connecting these holes. This serves as your top cutting line. Now measure down from this line the depth of the lintel, and draw a line on the wall at this level. Next, chip away the plaster along the lines, using a club hammer and bolster.

Before going any further, you must support the ceiling with adjustable props to carry the load of floors above.

Now remove a course of bricks where the lintel is to be fitted – first on the outside, then on the inside of the wall. This is done by breaking up a brick in the middle of the row, using a drill, then loosening bricks on either side, one at a time, using a hammer and cold chisel.

In this way you will get a horizontal gap, about 2¾ in wide (the thickness of a brick plus a layer of mortar). If this gap is not exactly in line with your cutting line, however, you will have to remove the row of bricks above it as well. Do not let this worry you: the bricks can be replaced once the lintel has been fitted.

Now insert the lintel into the opening. See that you do not fit it upside down: the flat side is the underside.

Force wedges under the lintel so that its upper edge fits tightly against the row of bricks above it. If more than one row of bricks has been removed, you will have to put a brick or something else above it, so

that it becomes firmly wedged at the required height. Hold your spirit level against the underside of the lintel and shift the wedges until the lintel is perfectly level.

Now you must mortar in around the 'ears' – the areas where the ends of the lintel rest on the wall on either side of the opening. Use a mixture of one part of cement to three of sand, and force the mortar in firmly under the lintel with your fingers. Also mortar back in place any bricks you may have had to remove from above the lintel.

Now leave the lintel for two days to allow the mortar to become good and hard. Finally, knock out the wall using the method described above.

Third Method

Use an angle grinder to cut the hole in your wall. This method is recommended, because the hole is made far more quickly and the end result is much neater. Also, shocks and plaster cracks are kept to a minimum.

Bear in mind that this could be a slightly more expensive method than the previous two, because the machine will probably have to be rented. Use an angle grinder that takes 9 in discs. Use a heavy-duty machine since lighter weight ones are not suitable.

You will have to buy about eight cutting discs. Make sure they are the kind designed for cutting bricks and stone.

You must observe strict safety rules.

3

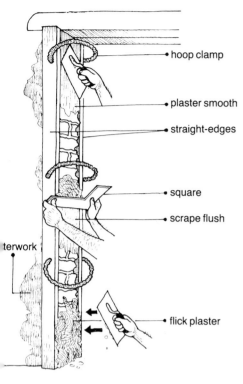

- hoop clamp
- plaster smooth
- straight-edges
- square
- scrape flush

terwork

- flick plaster

Using an angle grinder

Although the upper handle of the grinder can be attached to either side of the machine, always ensure that it is positioned so that the body of the grinder is between you and the blade. Wear safety glasses and a dust mask that covers your nose and mouth. Hold the grinder firmly when you switch it on – the high torque can force the cutting disc against your body unless you are braced for it.

Mark the position of the lintel on the outside and inside of the wall, as already described. Now cut the plaster and bricks free by running the cutting disc along the mortar lines above and below the course of bricks. Use a hammer drill to break up a brick in the middle of the row, then remove the rest with a club hammer and cold chisel. (Because its considerable weight makes this machine quite difficult to hold in position for a horizontal cut of this nature, you may prefer to set it aside and chip out the plaster with a bolster and club hammer instead. Then remove the bricks using a cold chisel and club hammer. If you have never worked with an angle grinder before, this latter method is probably the safest.)

Once the lintel has been mortared in position and the mortar has dried, you can cut the sides of the opening. Always begin a cut at the bottom and work upwards so the spinning blade does not obscure the cutting line in a layer of dust.

Push the cutting disc firmly, but slowly,

into the wall and move it slowly upwards. Repeat this on the inside of the wall. When one entire side of the opening has been cut through, hammer loose the bricks on that side up to about 24 in of the outline for the other side. Now make the second vertical cut. Then tap out the remaining bricks.

Warning: Do not cut both sides of the opening in succession. The whole chunk of wall thus freed could topple down when you start hammering, causing serious damage or injury.

Dust

A vast amount of dust is generated when you use an angle grinder. For the duration of the operation you should hang plastic sheeting, or old blankets or sheets, from the ceiling behind the wall on which you will be working. Also close all doors leading off the area and cover carpets and furniture.

Wiring and plumbing

Before you start cutting or chopping, make absolutely certain there are no electrical wires or water pipes hidden in that part of the wall. Get up into the ceiling and crawl as close as possible to the wall above the spot where you plan to cut the opening. If there are electrical conduits or pipes buried in the wall, these must be rerouted before demolition begins.

If the kitchen and a bathroom are on opposite sides of the planned door, or nearby, the chances are there will be water pipes in the wall at that point. Turn off the water supply at the main tap before you begin cutting. When you reach the pipe saw through it, and re-route it down and under the door at floor level – or call in a plumber to do the job.

Finishing

Once the opening has been completed, the edges must be plastered neatly. Before you begin this job, make yourself some simple spring clamps as an aid to holding the plastering battens against the edge of the opening as follows: saw four 24 in lengths of ½ in-diameter steel reinforcing rod, and bend each of them into a circular shape around a securely-based pole.

Now fill in all gaps where the old plaster or bricks have broken away on the wrong side of your cutting line, using a plaster mixture of one part cement to four parts sand. Take care not to make the mixture too wet, or it will not stick to the wall.

Next, place a straight-edge on either side of the wall and secure them there with the clamps you have made. Check the straight-edges with your spirit level, tapping them lightly with a hammer until they are exactly vertical.

Dampen the wall between the two planks. Now, starting at the bottom and working your way up, scoop up a lump of

plaster on the tip of your plastering trowel and press it against the face of the brickwork, pushing the trowel upwards against the edges of the guide battens.

Working from the top down this time, place the edge of a steel builder's square across the two straight-edges and, drawing it downwards, scrape the plaster level.

Finally, smooth the plaster with your plastering trowel. Wait for about an hour for it to harden a bit, then remove the two straight-edges. Use a corner trowel to round off the corners.

The lintel

It takes a little extra care to get the plaster to stick to the underside of the lintel.

First method

First flick dry cement against the underside of the lintel with your plastering trowel, then fix your straight-edges in position. Now throw the plaster mixture against the underside of the lintel and smooth it into place with the trowel, helping it to stick well by pressing it firmly upwards as you do so. Wait about two hours and then level the surface by scraping it with the steel square, in the same way as you did with the sides.

Second method

Buy a specially-formulated, ready-mixed plaster, which comes in a plastic tub. Stir it according to the manufacturer's instructions and spread it, layer by layer, on the underside of the lintel. This easy method is recommended, especially as the plaster will not fall off – a problem that gives most novices grey hairs when they work with ordinary plaster for the first time. This type of mixture is also recommended for any small plastering jobs around the house.

Hint

Sometimes, when you chop an opening in a wall, great chunks of plaster can break away in the wrong places. It is quite easy to repair the damage if you go about it the right way.

If the hole you have to repair is deeper than 1½ in, do not try to plaster the whole thing in one go, as the plaster will be too heavy and will fall off. Instead, tackle it in two stages. First, plaster the hole to about half its depth with the help of the straight-edges, then scratch criss-cross lines in the wet plaster, to allow the next layer to stick to it. Wait until this first layer is properly dry, then repeat the procedure.

If you have to patch deeper holes where bits of brick have been broken away, bed slivers of brick in mortar to fill out the hole and then plaster over as before.

12. PERGOLAS

Nowadays it can cost a fortune to have a prefabricated sun screen erected over your patio or your entertainment corner. A carport can be just as expensive. It is not at all necessary to spend so much. You can build superb pergolas, sun screens and a carport yourself, without much difficulty.

Pressure treated poles are suited to this purpose, particularly now that black, tarred poles are no longer your only choice. Poles treated with copper chrome-arsenate (Tanalith) have a natural colour that, together with vines, will blend attractively with the rest of your garden.

Another big advantage is that it is so easy to build with poles. It is actually a matter of planting the poles and nailing them fast. With the wide range of fixtures available today, it is not even necessary to drill holes.

If you do not like the gnarled appearance of natural poles, you can use treated poles that have been turned to a smooth finish. These are available in diameters from 2 to 8 in and lengths from 3 to 28 feet. With these poles you can make good-looking walls by planting them right up against each other, and the short ones look most attractive when they are used as edgings and low retaining walls.

When you order poles, remember that a pole's diameter is always measured at the thin end. If the measurement is stated as 3/4, it means the thin end is at least 3 in thick but not thicker than 4 in. When fences are built, the poles are often planted with the thin end alternately up and down, to prevent gaps.

For pergolas it is often not even necessary to plant the poles in concrete. Just dig the holes 2 feet deep and tamp the earth down firmly around the base of each pole.

If, however, you plan to fix roofing sheets to the top of the structure, it might be safer to fill the hole around the pole with concrete. Because of the danger of strong winds, the poles should also be bolted together.

Buy the poles the correct length. If you saw them off, the untreated ends are vulnerable to insects and fungus. Treat the ends with creosote or some other preservative and do not plant untreated ends in the ground.

Poles and timbers treated with Tanalith (they have a greenish colour) can be made more attractive out of doors by coating them with a solvent-based preservative stain. This brings out the wood colour, is resistant to water and does not flake off. Regular application is, however, necessary.

Construction methods
Do not, under any circumstances, use ordinary nails when you are building wooden structures in your yard. They rust, staining the wood, and will begin to loosen within a few years. Use galvanized nails which have corrugated surfaces that enable them to grip the wood very tightly.

In industrial or coastal areas where rust is a problem, every fixture must be painted before it is assembled, even when galvanized metal is used. First apply a galvanizing-cleaner, followed by a calcium plumbate metal primer for extra protection. Then paint the fixture with an iron oxide paint specially designed for use on galvanized iron roofs.

Use proprietary semi-circular log clamps to attach the horizontal poles to the tops of the vertical ones, or else cut simple halving joints and nail them.

Car shelters and pergolas can be built as free-standing structures, but it is just as good to attach one side to the side of the house. Hold a beam horizontally against the wall at the required height and place a spirit level on top of it to ensure that it is not skew.

At one end, drill a hole through the wood and into the wall. Push in a bolt to hold the beam temporarily in place. Repeat the process at the other end and put another temporary bolt in the hole. Now drill the rest of the holes through the beam and into the wall. In this way you can be certain that the holes in the beam and the wall correspond with each other.

Bolt the beam fast with fixtures such as masonry bolts, obtainable from hardware shops. Treat the bolt heads against rust and use a silicone sealant between the beam and the wall to keep the rain out.

Now nail the log clamps on top of the beam to hold the cross-poles in the correct position.

Timber
Use truss or joist hangers to support a pergola or carport against the wall of your house, and post anchor bases should be used to hold the support posts in position. The great advantage of these anchors is that they hold the posts a little off the ground, thereby preventing rot in the ends of the timber.

When support beams are to be erected in garden ground, a foundation must be

A pergola of preservative-treated poles makes a perfect canopy over the patio.

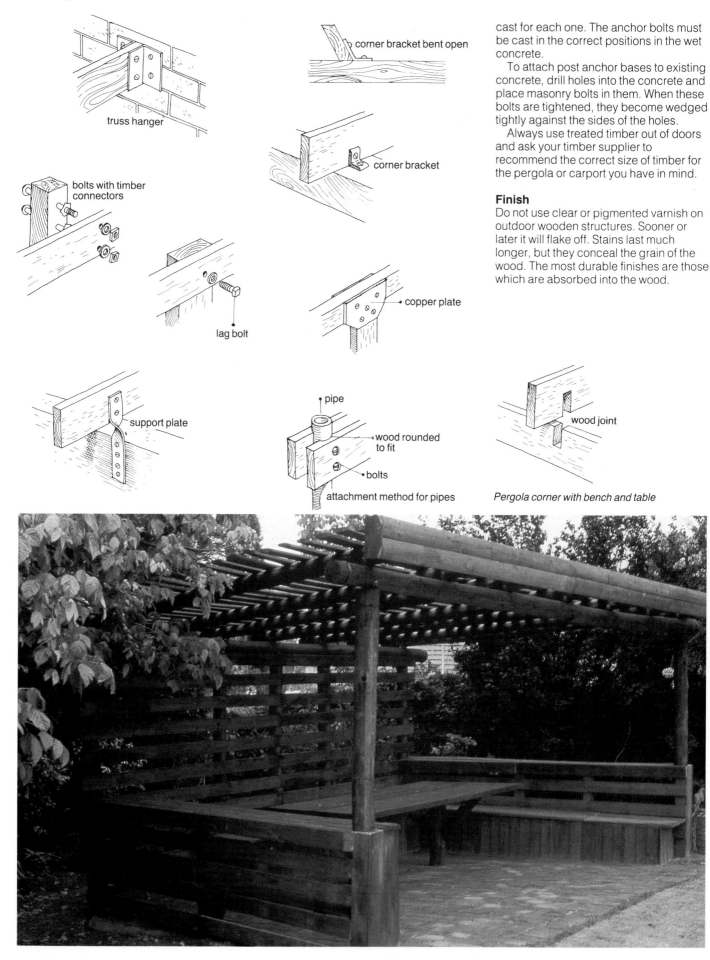

truss hanger

corner bracket bent open

bolts with timber connectors

corner bracket

lag bolt

copper plate

support plate

pipe

wood rounded to fit

bolts

attachment method for pipes

wood joint

Pergola corner with bench and table

cast for each one. The anchor bolts must be cast in the correct positions in the wet concrete.

To attach post anchor bases to existing concrete, drill holes into the concrete and place masonry bolts in them. When these bolts are tightened, they become wedged tightly against the sides of the holes.

Always use treated timber out of doors and ask your timber supplier to recommend the correct size of timber for the pergola or carport you have in mind.

Finish
Do not use clear or pigmented varnish on outdoor wooden structures. Sooner or later it will flake off. Stains last much longer, but they conceal the grain of the wood. The most durable finishes are those which are absorbed into the wood.

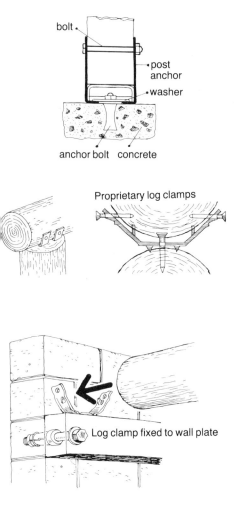

bolt

post anchor

washer

anchor bolt   concrete

Proprietary log clamps

Log clamp fixed to wall plate

Unusual bamboo pergola with large log sections used as floor and pathway.

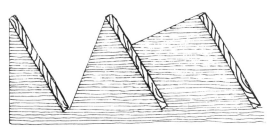

sun directly overhead

late afternoon

Square planks (laths) provide little shade if they are placed too far apart.

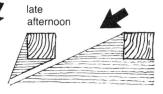

Planks placed on edge give much more shade.

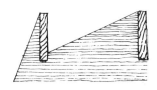

Planks placed at an angle give the best shade of all.

13. ALL ABOUT CONCRETE

You can use concrete to good effect for patios, pathways, driveways and other garden projects. Colouring the concrete or giving it a special texture can produce a very attractive end result. All the basic knowledge required for working with concrete is supplied here. When you have read this chapter, you will be ready to tackle your first project.

Cement, sand and stone are the basis of any masonry and concrete work. The main difference between ordinary mortar and concrete is that mortar is made of cement, sand and water, while concrete has stone added to it. These four constituents are discussed below.

Cement
Portland cement, which is used in practically all building work, hardens by the reaction of chemicals with water. Too little or too much water weakens this reaction and affects the eventual strength of the mortar or concrete. Mortar or concrete that is allowed to dry too quickly is also weakened. This is why concrete must be kept damp while it is setting.

When you store cement, always bear in mind that the cement in the bag will react with any moisture in the air or ground. This is why you should store the bags on sheets of plastic and cover them with plastic.

The need to store cement correctly is illustrated by the following: In an airtight drum, cement will retain its full strength for three years. If you store it in a dry place on plastic and cover it well with more plastic, it will lose 20 per cent of its strength within three months and 30 per cent in six months; after two years it will have only half its original strength.

Always use fresh cement when structural strength is important. For non-structural work, like building in your garden, you can increase the quantity of cement slightly to compensate for any reduction in strength.

Sand
The type of sand you use plays an important role in the quality of your concrete or mortar mixture. As a novice builder, you would be well-advised to order or collect your sand from a local builders' supply. Try looking in your Yellow Pages, and ask a dealer to recommend a good type of sand for your particular job (concrete or bricklaying), and compare prices.

Grain size: The grain size of good concrete sand varies from dust to about ¼ in. If the grains are all the same size, it is not as easily workable.

Different sands are available in different parts of the country, but you can safely assume that any sand you are offered has been correctly graded as sharp sand (for concrete) or soft sand (for bricklaying and rendering). The only major difference between sands from different areas is likely to be the colour, which of course will affect the final colour of the mortar.

Unwashed sea sand should not be used because the salt in it causes the reinforcing in concrete to rust and produces a white deposit on plaster work.

No building sand should contain organic material.

Concrete stone (Aggregate)
Crushed concrete stone of about ¾ in is usually used by professionals, but ½ in is best for do-it-yourselfers because it is easier to work with smaller stones.

The following is a good rule of thumb to determine the size of your stone: the diameter of the stones should not be more than one third of the final thickness of the concrete.

Check your mixture as you go: there is too much stone if they stick out above the surface after it has been poured and tamped down. Scratch the surface of the wet concrete with a finger nail. If the stones are more than a few millimetres below the surface, you have used too much sand in your mixture. Concrete made with very fine sand needs more stone in it, and vice versa.

Water
Water is the catalyst which starts the chemical reaction that binds the cement, sand and stone together. The golden rule is: if you cannot drink the water, do not use it for concrete work.

Too much water is the first thing you have to guard against when you – or particularly your helpers – mix concrete or mortar. Concrete is usually made too sloppy, simply because it is easier to work with like that. Too much water not only weakens the mixture, but also causes the cement to float to the surface, which weakens the lower layers of concrete even more.

The less water you use in your mixture, the stronger your concrete or mortar will be and the more difficult it will be to work with this 'stiff' mixture. Too little water results in concrete that is porous, and weaker when it has set.

A general guide is to add just enough water to bind all the ingredients and make a plastic mixture that slides rather reluctantly from your spade when you hold it at an angle. If you do add too much water you must compensate by adding dry ingredients in the correct proportions, and mixing them in thoroughly. Beware of wet sand: it requires far less water than you would normally use.

Slab thickness
The following minimum slab thicknesses are recommended for concrete:
Garden paths and patios: 3 in
Floors: 4 in
Carport floors, driveways: 4 in
Bricks or paving slabs on concrete: 1½ in

Left: This garden path has been tastefully designed with small stones set in concrete. Right: Stones set into concrete can be used decoratively or to provide a non-slip surface for a driveway.

Strip foundations: 6 in thick and at least twice the width of the masonry.

Mixtures

All the ingredients must be measured by volume in containers. For small mixes where the final quantity is not critical, follow the formulae for mixture 1 in the table and use any handy container such as a domestic bucket for measuring quantities: it is the relative amounts of each component that must be in the correct proportions.

For larger mixes where the final volume is critical, use the formulae based on 1 bag of cement. To measure out the sand and aggregate volumes, use either a standard builder's bucket which holds approximately 3 gallons (14 litres, or 0,014cu m), or a standard navvy barrow holding 3cu ft (0,85cu m).

To make the concrete more workable, a plasticizer can be added. Mix it in according to the manufacturer's instructions.

☐ *Mixture 1* gives the strongest concrete and is suitable for driveways, garage floors and reinforced concrete.
☐ *Mixture 2* is a medium strength concrete and is suitable for pathways, patios, edgings and steps.
☐ *Mixture 3* is suitable for all foundations.

The purpose of the concrete best determines the mixture. To make a strong mixture and then cast too thick a slab is simply a waste of money, time and labour.

How to hand-mix concrete

To mix a sizable quantity of concrete by hand is certainly not child's play. A cubic yard of concrete weighs 2.4 tons – and you have to lift those 2.4 tons at least 12 times with your spade to get it properly mixed, after which you still have to move it around in a wheelbarrow.

The best advice is to get help – preferably helpers who realize what is involved. If at all possible, the job should be completed in a single day. Start early, long before the sun begins to get too hot.

Do your mixing on a clean, hard surface, like a concrete slab, or lay a number of bricks to act as a mixing surface. Do not mix more concrete than you can use in half an hour.

There are several methods of mixing concrete by hand. Some people, for example, first measure out the aggregate, others start with cement and sand and then add the aggregate and water, and so on. The following method is recommended because it is the best way to ensure that all the ingredients are thoroughly mixed.

Concrete steps finished with a grit surface.

Mixture 1 (strong — drives etc)

	Cement	Sand	¾ in aggregate	All-in aggregate	Yield
	1 bucket	1½ buckets	2½ buckets	—	3½ buckets
or	1 bucket	—	—	3½ buckets	3½ buckets
	1 bag (100 lbs)	1¾ cu ft (150 lbs)	3 cu ft (300 lbs)	—	4 cu ft
or	1 bag (100 lbs)	—	—	4 cu ft (500 lbs)	4 cu ft

Mixture 2 (medium — general-purpose use)

	Cement	Sand	¾ in aggregate	All-in aggregate	Yield
	1 bucket	2 buckets	3 buckets	—	4 buckets
or	1 bucket	—	—	4 buckets	4 buckets
	1 bag (100 lbs)	2½ cu ft (225 lbs)	3.7 cu ft (400 lbs)	—	5.3 cu ft
or	1 bag (100 lbs)	—	—	5 cu ft (650 lbs)	5.3 cu ft

Mixture 3 (standard — foundations etc)

	Cement	Sand	¾ in aggregate	All-in aggregate	Yield
	1 bucket	2½ buckets	3½ buckets	—	5 buckets
or	1 bucket	—	—	5 buckets	5 buckets
	1 bag (100 lbs)	3 cu ft (275 lbs)	4.3 cu ft (450 lbs)	—	6.5 cu ft
or	1 bag (100 lbs)	—	—	6 cu ft (725 lbs)	6.5 cu ft

First measure out the sand, and flatten the pile with your spade. Now pour the cement on top and flatten it out, too. Now push the spade well down under the sand and tip it over, throwing the mixture into a pile in the centre. In this way, keep moving around the pile, repeating the operation until the mixture has an even grey colour.

Flatten the pile again and make a little hollow in the middle of it. Pour in some of the water and mix it all as before. Add water until the mixture looks like sloppy porridge. Flatten the heap and pour the stone on top of it. Mix as before and add a little water if the mixture appears a bit dry.

The mixture is ready when it has an even grey colour and there are no unmixed ingredients left over.

Concrete-mixer

For larger projects it is definitely worth hiring a concrete mixer. Make sure everything is ready to start mixing before the mixer arrives, so you can return it as quickly as possible.

When using a concrete mixer, first put the stone into the drum, with a little water. This cleans the drum and prevents lumps of concrete sticking to the blades inside. Now add the cement, followed by the sand and the rest of the water.

Pouring

Before the concrete is poured into place, the trench or ground under the shuttering (see page 72) must be thoroughly wetted to prevent the dry ground drawing water from the concrete and weakening it. As soon as the concrete is in place, it must be prodded and stirred with a stick or heavy steel pole, particularly in the corners, to get rid of any air bubbles and ensure a dense, even layer of concrete. Do not overdo this, however, or the cement and sand will begin to float to the surface.

After care

All new concrete must be kept damp for at least five days (seven days or longer if it is very cold) to prevent drying out and cracking. In cold weather the concrete should be covered with sacks or grass to prevent the temperature dropping below 50 °F.

Moisture loss can be prevented by spreading sand, straw or sacking on the concrete and keeping it wet. Another method is to cover the concrete with plastic, or to spray it each day with a garden hose.

Always remember that the moisture determines the hardness of the concrete.

Coloured concrete

Concrete and mortar can be coloured in the mixing stage by adding yellow, brown, red, pink, grey, blue or green pigment. Buy the best quality pigment – one that is based on metallic oxide.

Normally you need between 10 and 30 lbs of pigment for each cubic yard of concrete, and between 17 and 30 lbs per cubic yard of mortar. The blue and green pigments tend to bleach and should not be used outdoors, unless the manufacturer is prepared to give you a guarantee.

Make trial batches and allow them to dry before you decide how much pigment to add. Mix the pigment with cement and sand and sift it a few times through a sieve just big enough to allow the sand through.

When pastel colours are required, you can add the appropriate pigment to a mixture of white Portland cement, a whitish sand and stone. Ready-mixed pigmented white cement is also available in a wide range of shades. This offers an easy solution if you want to avoid using grey cement in your garden. You merely have to mix the concrete to obtain an even colour throughout.

Preparation for laying concrete

If there is one material that is perfectly suited to the do-it-yourself enthusiast who wants to tackle building projects in his yard, it is concrete. It is as versatile as clay. You can make a wet concrete mixture and pour it into any mould to produce a product that will last for years and years in all sorts of weather, and keep looking good without any maintenance work.

The 'looking good' part is the problem. To most people, concrete means a cold, lifeless grey mass which – for aesthetic reasons – should be eliminated as far as possible, particularly in a garden.

This is a misconception. You can colour concrete by using the right colour cement, stone and sand, or by adding pigment at the mixing stage. You can give it interesting textures and patterns by using an ordinary brush or yard broom. Or you can give it a completely different look by embedding stones or colourful gravel in the surface.

The only demand that concrete makes on you is that you use it correctly. In this and previous chapters you have learned the basic principles of working with concrete: how to level your ground and get the correct slope so rainwater will drain away, plus the right concrete mixtures and the best way to mix concrete.

In this chapter you will also learn how to place and compact concrete properly

1. Stretch your builder's lines to indicate the edges of the path, and dig out strips along each side to allow for the shuttering.

2. Hold a sledgehammer or brick against the back with your foot, to absorb the shock of the hammer blows.

3. One side of the shuttering must be lower, so the rainwater will drain away.

4. Scrape the concrete with a straight-edge until it is level with the top of the shuttering.

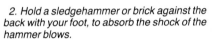

5. Smooth the surface of the concrete with a float.

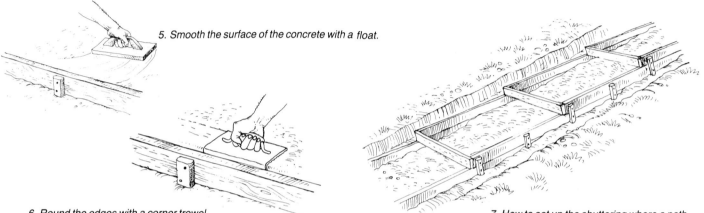

6. Round the edges with a corner trowel.

7. How to set up the shuttering where a path must be stepped.

and neatly in position – and how to give concrete a different look by applying various finishing techniques. These techniques are suitable for all above-ground structures in your garden – from a pathway to a patio or a serviceable floor for a barbecue. The choice of final finish is yours: a plain concrete slab without any flourishes to serve as a parking place for your car, a warm-coloured concrete slab with a textured surface, or a surface that is framed with paving bricks, paving stones or just ordinary bricks.

The three golden rules of all masonry work are: everything must be at right angles, level and vertical (or plumb). If you think it does not really matter if your patio or barbecue is 'a little bit out' or your path is not quite the same width all the way, you will most certainly regret it, and the end result will be spoiled. If you lay a concrete slab that is not square or at right angles, it might not actually be so drastic in itself. But every bit of building work you do later on that patio or path, or alongside it, will be skew and crooked because all your measurements will have been made from a crooked base-line. And you will battle like mad trying to get bricks laid straight or to fit in things like drainage channels neatly.

So study page 83 carefully to learn how to set out a square.

Edging

All concrete must have some sort of neat edging, whether it be the walls of the foundation trench, a little wall consisting of one or two courses of bricks, or wooden shuttering. This forms the outline of the concrete structure and prevents the wet concrete from flowing away when it is poured. To achieve a concrete slab that is equally thick at all points and to ensure that rainwater will drain away without forming puddles, you should be particularly careful when erecting the edging, making certain that it is perfectly square. This is the most important aspect of all concrete work.

Another important point is that the ground beyond the edging must have the correct slope to carry away rainwater. See Chapter 3 for instructions on how to do this.

Shuttering

In the chapter describing how to build a patio by laying bricks on sand (page 53), several methods are shown for edging bricks or concrete. The method described here is the one used most often when an

ordinary concrete slab is required. You can use this method when throwing a plain concrete path or patio, or where the concrete will serve as a base for bricks, crazy paving, slate or any other paving material.

Concrete paths

Even an ordinary garden path must have a slope to carry away rainwater in the direction in which it will do the least damage, so ensure that the shuttering is always a shade lower on the side to which you want the water to run. To do this, check the levels of the two sides of the shuttering at regular intervals. If you want the water to run to the left, allow the bubble in the spirit level to just touch the line on the right.

Another way is to tape a thin piece of wood to the bottom of one end of the spirit level with masking tape, thereby automatically 'building in' a slope. See page 21 for how this is done.

A dead-straight garden path seldom looks attractive, particularly in an informal garden. To make your path meander, you should create smooth curves in the right places. All you need are strips of hardboard (¼ in or two thicknesses of

8. Finishing – sprinkle grit or fine stones on the concrete surface if you want to create a different texture.

9. Tamp the stones down into the concrete with a plank.

10. Use a float to tamp stubborn stones down.

11. Brush excess cement away from the stones with running water and a broom.

12. Another way of adding texture: brush patterns into the concrete with a stiff yard broom.

⅛ in), bent and held in position with pegs driven in every 6 in or so against the inside and outside of the board.

Hint
Hardboard bends a little more easily if it is first soaked in water for a while.

First, knock pegs into the ground to indicate the exact width of the pathway and stretch a builder's line between the pegs. Make the path about 3½ feet wide – just wide enough to allow two people to pass each other.

You will need to dig deep enough to make provision for the concrete and bricks or paving stones.

First dig a narrow trench along the outside of the lines for the shuttering. Then remove the lines and dig out the rest of the earth from the middle.

The planks you use for the shuttering can be a little narrower than the thickness of the concrete, because the shuttering is usually raised a bit here and there with wedges or little blocks of wood to ensure that it is level.

Now replace the builder's lines and hold the shuttering planks in position, so that their inside edges are directly below the line. Hammer in square pegs with

sharpened points at more-or-less three-foot intervals along the outer surfaces of the planks. Now secure the planks by hammering nails through the pegs on the outside, and into the planks. (To prevent splitting and other problems, it is a good idea to drill pilot holes through the pegs before hammering them into the ground.) Hold a brick or a sledgehammer against the inside of the plank to absorb the shock of the hammer blows and prevent the pegs from shifting.

If the shuttering is not good and firm, you can hammer in pegs or reinforcing rods tightly against the inside of the planks here and there. Because these will remain in position, they should be driven in to at least ¾ in below the top of the shuttering.

The above method is only suitable for softish ground. For stony ground you will have to build an independent, right-angled framework. Place this shuttering in position below the builder's line and hammer in reinforcing rods instead of wooden pegs.

Do not be concerned if the rods get bent by stones in the ground. All you need to do is knock wedges in between the rods and the framework.

When the shuttering is removed, there

will be gaps left in the concrete between the various slabs, but these need not be a problem: they can either serve as expansion joints or be filled with sand or mortar once the concrete has dried. Another way to break the monotony of plain concrete is to allow a bit of greenery to grow in the gaps.

Alternatively, the shuttering itself provides a pleasing contrast in texture with the concrete, and can be left in place, providing it has been properly treated against woodrot. In any case, it is important to remember that an expansion joint should be built in every one-and-a-half times the width of the path.

If you find knocking in the wooden pegs a real battle, you can mix a bit of mortar and place it against the shuttering here and there to hold it in place. Wait until it has set before throwing the concrete, and chip it out when you wish to remove the shuttering.

Another point to bear in mind: if your ground is so hard that you cannot hammer a wooden peg into it, you probably do not need a concrete base for your patio or pathway, anyway. It will be just as good, and far cheaper, to lay your paving blocks on ordinary sand. See Chapter 11 for how this is done.

Steps

If your ground is lightly contoured, without any pronounced hills or valleys, the concrete you pour will simply follow the contours of the earth. But when you have a steeper slope, you will have to cast steps. All you have to do is to let the shuttering overlap in the right places. Study the sketch to see how this is done; also see the chapter on steps on page 45. Any hollows that may develop where the steps are planned should be filled with earth, stones or rubble and tamped down firmly before the concrete is cast.

Do not just make the steps randomly. Space them evenly. This way, they look better and are easier to walk on.

Patio shuttering

The same basic shuttering technique is used to cast an ordinary concrete slab, a concrete patio or the concrete base for paving stones or bricks. The only difference is that the surface is larger.

Of course, for larger areas you should pay particular attention to correct drainage and expansion joints, to prevent the slab cracking due to shrinkage or expansion. Indoors – for example when you are laying a concrete floor for a garage – shrinkage and expansion present no problems, but it is quite a different matter when a large area of concrete like a patio is exposed to the sun, wind and weather.

To make provision for expansion, no outdoor concrete slabs should be cast in blocks bigger than 10 x 10 feet.

Equally important is the height of the patio. Its surface must be lower than the damp-proof course in the walls of your house, to prevent damp rising into your walls. The safest height is two brick thicknesses below the damp-proof course. (This applies to all outdoor structures you build against the walls of your house – even a flower bed.)

Ensure that your ground is smooth and has the required slope (see page 54) and that the straight sides of your patio are at right angles to the walls of your house, before you begin with shuttering work.

First put down the planks that form the outer borders, and then the partitions. If the partitions are supported by pegs, the pegs must be set about 8 in below the top of the partition, to prevent their sticking out above the surface of the concrete.

The partitions offer another benefit: you do not have to lay the whole slab in one day. Sections not completed can be finished the following day or weekend, without weakening the slab at all.

If the partitions are to be removed, they can be pulled or lifted out carefully a few hours later, while the concrete is still reasonably soft. Fill the gaps with mortar or just leave them if you plan to lay paving or bricks on top of the concrete.

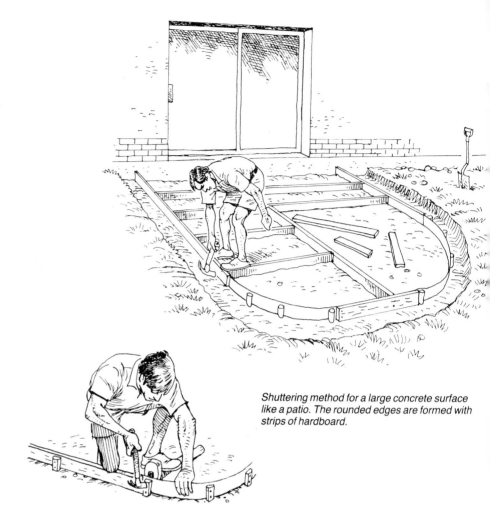

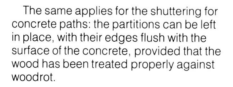

Shuttering method for a large concrete surface like a patio. The rounded edges are formed with strips of hardboard.

The same applies for the shuttering for concrete paths: the partitions can be left in place, with their edges flush with the surface of the concrete, provided that the wood has been treated properly against woodrot.

The pouring

When the shuttering is ready, you should make pathways for your wheelbarrow. Use old planks for these, raising them on bricks where they have to clear the sides of the shuttering.

Before the concrete is poured into place, the trench and ground under the shuttering must be thoroughly wetted to prevent the dry ground from drawing water from the concrete and weakening it.

Tip the wheelbarrow-load of concrete out in the furthest corner and flatten the heap with your spade. Prod the concrete with a stout stick or iron rod to make it settle and to get rid of bubbles so as to ensure a dense, even layer of concrete. Do not overdo this, however, or the cement and sand will begin to float to the surface. Then tamp and scrape the surface of the concrete with your straight-edge to get it level with the top of the shuttering.

The straight-edge should be long enough to ensure that it always rests on both sides of the shuttering. In this way you are ensuring that the surface of the concrete can be scraped down to exactly the level of the shuttering.

Use the straight-edge in a sawing motion, drawing it towards you. If it is too short to reach right across the shuttering, you can place a 'height gauge' in a convenient place in the middle of the section and rest the straight-edge on this to check the level of the concrete. A wooden peg, hammered in so it sticks up to the exact level of the shuttering, is ideal for this. Without this peg you could easily scrape away too much concrete in the middle of the section.

Finally, tamp the concrete flat with the side of the straight-edge to remove the scrape marks and to embed any loose stones that may have popped up during the scraping.

Finishes
Method 1

As soon as the shiny layer of water disappears from the top of the concrete, it is time to rub the surface smooth. For this you use a wooden float, which is just an oblong piece of wood with a handle. Run this float back and forth across the surface of the concrete, using just enough pressure to smooth it without letting the float stick fast. Sprinkle a little water on if the concrete becomes too dry and place scaffolding planks across the shuttering to kneel on while you are smoothing.

After this, the edges should be rounded with a corner trowel to ensure smooth edges once the shuttering is removed. The corner trowel has a rounded edge which is rubbed back and forth between the concrete and the shuttering. Use the wooden float again to get rid of the shiny marks left by the metal corner trowel.

The texture obtained by this method is nicely smooth, but not so smooth that it becomes slippery when wet. If you use a steel plastering float – a steel rectangle with a handle – the concrete will be too smooth for outdoor use.

Method 2
To create an interesting surface texture, smooth the concrete with the wooden float as before, then draw a stiff yard broom across the surface in straight lines. Another interesting texture can be obtained by making diagonal patterns with a broom, or by using it to form zig-zags or wavy lines across the surface.

Method 3
Sprinkle grit, gravel or other fine stones on the concrete after you have smoothed it. Select the colour and texture of the stones with care: if suitable ones are not available from your building supplier, make enquiries through local quarries or even at monumental masons, either of whom should be able to offer you a choice of suitable decorative aggregates.

To make sure the stones stick firmly to the concrete, it is better to use a little more sand than usual in the concrete mixture.

Get a helper to hold one end of a good, thick plank and tamp the stones down evenly into the concrete surface. Take care to get an even layer of stones. Bare patches are the commonest problem with this finishing method.

To prevent the concrete drying too fast, you will have to divide the surface area into manageable sections, then see that the stones are tamped into place as quickly as possible.

The tops of the stones should barely stick up above the level of the concrete. Use the wooden float to tamp down any stubborn stones.

About eight hours later, when the concrete has set nicely, the surface should be brushed lightly to remove any surplus cement around the stones. Spray a gentle stream of water onto the concrete while you brush. A few hours later you will be able to rinse off a fine layer of cement powder from the stones by spraying gently with the hose again.

Lastly: Do not simply rush in and attempt to pebble finish a huge area of concrete at a time. First mix a little concrete and practise on it. This test patch can easily be chipped away before it dries completely.

Note:
It is most important that you know how to treat newly-laid concrete; see page 69, 'After care'.

Brick-paving is an attractive and durable finish for concrete steps and is also suitable for a driveway or patio.

Bricks on concrete

Bricks can be laid on concrete in a wide variety of patterns to create paths or patios. And if there is a patch of unsightly bare concrete anywhere in your garden, you can easily disguise it with paving bricks.

Remember that it is not always necessary to lay bricks on concrete. In most cases they can simply be laid on a bed of ordinary sand. On page 55 you can see how this is done.

Always lay the bricks out on the ground in the desired pattern before excavating the base and filling it with concrete (see page 56). In this way you can avoid having to cut bricks unnecessarily.

Sweep the concrete base clean before laying the bricks on it. The joints between the bricks should be about ½ in wide. Use a piece of plank or hardboard as a spacer. If the bricks are to be laid in straight lines, use a builder's line beside each row, as bricks that are laid skew do not look good. Just wind each of the ends of a length of string around a brick to hold it in position, then place another couple of bricks on top to hold each firmly in place.

Remember never to lay a brick actually touching the line – there must always be a gap of about $1/_{32}$ in to prevent the string being stretched out of alignment.

When the bricks are laid in position, dry mortar consisting of one part cement to four parts sand is poured into the joints from a tin can. Prod the mixture down using the spacer, and add more if necessary.

Use a soft brush to remove all the cement that has fallen on top of the bricks. Now direct a light spray of water over the bricks to wet the mixture. Add more of the dry mixture to any places where the mortar has sunk. Leave for about five minutes, then give it another sprinkling to ensure that the mixture is thoroughly wet.

Smooth the joints with a pointing tool or mastic trowel. Finally, wipe any stray cement from the bricks, using a damp sponge, to prevent ugly marks.

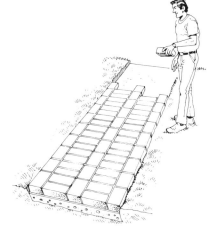

1. A brick-paved path laid on a concrete base.

2. A dry sand-cement mixture is poured in between the joints.

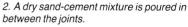

3. Spray lightly with water to allow the mixture to set.

Pebble paving

Another way to give new or old concrete a different texture is to 'pebble pave' it. In this process, small, brightly-coloured natural pebbles are bonded together with resin in a concrete mixer and spread onto the concrete surface in an even layer about ½ in thick. As the resin sets very fast, however, this is not recommended as a do-it-yourself project. There are contractors throughout the country who specialize in laying this type of finish, and will be happy to give a quotation.

The mixture is spread without any joints and the final result looks rather like a carpet. Apart from its attractive colour, a benefit of this material is the fact that it can be laid on almost any firm surface, including concrete, brick paving, crazy paving, slate or tar. Because it provides a good, skid-proof surface, even when wet, it is ideal for use as a swimming pool surround or pathway.

The carpeted look of good pebble paving.

Crazy paving

Crazy paving, whether it is of natural stone, slate or river stones with flattish surfaces, is a good way of decorating concrete surfaces like patios and garden paths. It is serviceable, attractive and surprisingly easy to lay.

Stepping stones

The easiest method of all is simply to make a hollow in the ground and place the flat stones – or even slabs of wood – on top of a layer of clean sand so they can serve as stepping stones across the lawn. First place the stones in position on top of the ground to see what they will look like, before digging the holes.

You can even cast your own stepping stones in concrete. Use your garden hose to indicate the outlines of the pathway. Dig holes about 4 in deep with a garden spade, making sure their outlines form the shape of the required stepping stones. Dig the holes about a pace apart and use a concrete mixture of one part cement, two parts sand and three parts aggregate. Colour the concrete as required before you mix it.

Shape the surfaces of your 'stepping stones' with a trowel, a piece of plank, or even your hands.

Laying crazy paving over concrete

Crazy paving is a good way to decorate a new or existing concrete slab or footpath. If the surface is too smooth or very dirty, you should first roughen it by chipping little holes all over it with a pick, so the mortar will have a good gripping surface. If the stone slabs are very porous, wet them or soak them in water to prevent them from drawing water out of the mortar mixture.

Lay out two or three of the stone slabs to see how the shapes fit together. If they make a good fit, put them to one side in the same position in which they will be laid.

Now make your mortar mixture, consisting of one part cement and three parts building sand. The mixture should be nice and firm, so that the stones do not sink too deeply into it. Brush off any sand or clay adhering to the stones so that they will stick firmly to the mortar.

Now sprinkle a little dry cement powder onto the concrete surface and mix it by painting it with a wet brush. This layer of undiluted cement ensures that the mortar will form a good bond with the concrete. Sprinkle only enough cement for two or three stones, or you will mess up the whole area.

Now place a layer of about ¾ in of mortar onto the concrete base, lower a stone onto this and tap it gently with a rubber hammer to embed it firmly in the mixture. Use your spirit level often to ensure that the stones are level and that

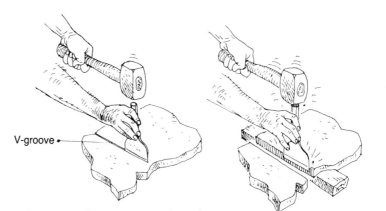

V-groove

1. Some types of paving stone can be cut by making a cutting line with a bolster.

2. This is how paving stones are laid on a concrete base.

there is the correct slope for drainage. The joints between the stones should be about ½ in wide.

If one of the stones sinks lower than its surroundings, lift it and place more mortar under it.

Once they are laid, leave the stones for a day or two, then fill in the joints between them with mortar. See that the mortar fills the gaps well by prodding it down with the edge of your trowel. Smooth the joints neatly with the trowel or a piece of wood and wipe away any stray cement immediately with a rag or sponge, to avoid staining the stones.

Cutting

Crazy paving and slate can be cut, but the type of stone determines the best way to do this. Try the following test. Place the stone flat on the ground and chisel out a shallow groove along the cutting line, using a bolster or cold chisel. Now place a straight plank under the stone so the chiselled groove hangs over by a millimetre or so. Place the chisel in the middle of the groove and give it a sharp hammer blow.

If you cannot cut the stone satisfactorily this way, you will have to rent an angle grinder. Ensure that you use the cutting

disc intended for stone and brick. Be warned: if you intend to cut a large number of stones this way, it could be an expensive business. Hard stones, and particularly thick slate, soon demolish the cutting discs – and they are not cheap.

Natural stone

A path made with smooth natural stone is attractive, but can become slippery and hard to walk on when it is wet. A good alternative is to use the natural stones to break up the monotony of a concrete path by having an oblong strip of stones embedded in the surface at regular intervals.

They can also be used to break the monotony of an area paved with concrete paving blocks. Just leave out a block here and there and fill the gaps with natural stones. If the blocks have already been laid, odd ones can be removed. Chisel them out if they cannot be lifted easily. Dig a hole deep enough for the stones and place shuttering or other suitable edging in position. When you are pouring the concrete, do not fill the shuttering right to the top, or the concrete will overflow when the stones are pressed into the surface. Fill any gaps with concrete and rub the joints smooth.

14. FISH PONDS

A fish pond, with or without its own fountain or even a small waterfall, will endow any garden with life, movement, a sense of coolness and a restful charm. It is not particularly expensive and you can build it quite easily yourself. Actually, the only skill you need is the ability to dig a hole.

The easiest and cheapest method of all is simply to line the hole with a special pool liner and then to lay a surround of paving slabs or natural stone round the perimeter. PVC liners are the cheapest type, but have a fairly short life expectancy. Butyl rubber is the best, but is also the most expensive.

Ponds built of concrete or bricks are not recommended as they require a considerable amount of work and tend to leak too easily.

Positioning
Do not build your pond too close to large trees, because it could be damaged by the roots, and the leaves will foul the water. Ensure that the pond becomes one of the focal points of the garden by positioning it where it can easily be seen from your living room or patio. Its effect is lost if it can only be seen by people heading for the front door. Also, make sure that the pond will get enough sunlight throughout the year.

Construction methods
Mark the outlines of the pond using a hose, a row of bricks or a track of sand. Avoid complicated shapes and include a rockery or slope as part of the pond plan. This is also a good way to use the excavated earth.

The pond need be no deeper than 1½ feet. Water deeper than this tends to stagnate rather easily.

Around the edges, form a shallower ledge where you can position water plants in submerged pots. These plants will soften the outlines of the pond. Choose them with care: shallow water plants for the edges and deep water plants grouped in the centre.

Dig the sides with a slope of about 60° to prevent their crumbling away when you position the lining. Place your straight-edge across the hole and put the spirit level on it. Scrape away ground where necessary, to ensure that the edges are absolutely level.

This fish pond was built with a surround of railroad ties.

Measure the maximum depth of the pond, and add twice this figure to the area (length by width) of the pond when calculating how big a liner you will need to buy.

Rake level a layer of clean building sand about 1¼ in deep over the bottom of the hole, then roll the liner out across the hole. Allow an overlap of about 6 in all round, and pleat the liner where necessary so it follows the curves of the hole smoothly.

Stand bricks on the liner edges to hold it in place. Fill the hole slowly with water, releasing the bricks one by one as the liner is stretched into place.

Now spread some sand on top of the liner round the edge of the hole, and lay the edging stones or paving blocks on this. They can also be embedded in a layer of mortar if you prefer. Use a mixture of one part cement to four parts sand.

If you have enough water plants to supply oxygen, the water need never be replaced, even if it does become a bit greenish. It will certainly not harm the fish.

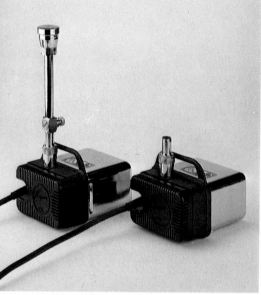

A submersible pump that can operate a fountain and circulate water over a miniature waterfall.

Pre-formed ponds

Ready-made ponds of Fiberglass or rigid plastic can also be used. Tip the pond over and draw around it to mark the outline on the ground. Now turn it the right way up and place it in the middle of the outline. Draw around the bottom to mark that. Dig the hole about 4 in wider than indicated by the outline you have drawn.

As before, rake a 1¼ in layer of clean sand over the bottom of the hole and place the ready-made pond on it. Use a spirit level to ensure that the sides are perfectly level.

Fill it about a tenth full before you begin filling in the ground around the sides. The water will prevent the pond shifting about. Now build the edging.

Fountains

A wide range of submersible, plastic water pumps is available, capable of creating almost any spray pattern you can imagine. Such a pump can also be linked to a statue, or statues, of your choice. Or you can use a pump to send a continuous stream of water to a higher level, to form a waterfall.

The pump is simply placed on a couple of bricks in the middle of the pond to prevent its sucking in too much sediment. Being plastic, it is waterproof and rust-free, and it is connected to the domestic electricity supply. The manufacturer's wiring instructions must be followed very carefully.

Water pumps that can be positioned above ground, alongside the pond, are also available.

Lighting

Garden lights are available with sturdy spikes attached to them for sticking into the ground.

Some submersible pumps even have their own built-in underwater lights for added effect.

Lastly: always remember that babies and toddlers can drown as easily in a fish pond as they can in a swimming pool.

1. Mark out the shape of the pond using a garden hose.

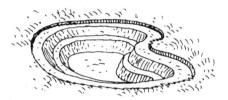

2. Dig the hole and make provision for two levels on which potted plants can be placed.

3. Lay the pond liner in position.

4. Partially fill the pond and lay the edging paving stones on a layer of mortar.

Layout of a fish pond with a fountain and waterfall.

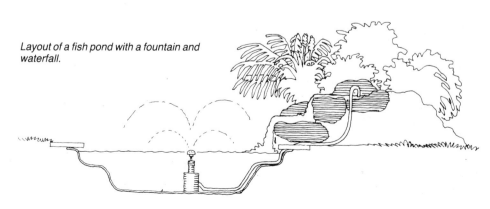

Detail of the edging pavers

15. MEASURE AND FIT

Here are a few handy guidelines to help you work out just how many bricks and how much building material you will need to complete a project in your garden.

Bricks

For a single (half-brick) wall, you will need 6 bricks for every square foot. For a double (one-brick) wall you will need 12 bricks per ft².

Sand

You will require 1¼ cubic yards of sand for every 5 standard 100 lb bags of Portland cement.

Cement

For every square foot of brickwork (6 bricks) you will need about a fifth of a bag of cement. One 100 lb bag of ready-mixed mortar will lay about 50 bricks. Always estimate the total wall area first, then subtract the area of any openings.

Patios

For laying a patio, you will need about 18 bricks per square foot if they are laid flat without pointing, and 26 if they are laid on edge. Reduce these figures by about 10 per cent if they are to be laid with pointing in between.

When trying to work out the area of a complicated shape, for example a patio with rounded corners and openings for trees or flower beds, it is best to draw everything to scale on graph paper, letting each square represent a given size, say one square foot. Count the squares, estimate the area of the half-squares and add the figures to get the grand total.

Concrete

To calculate the number of cubic yards of concrete you will need, measure out the surface area of the planned slab, then multiply the length by the breadth by the thickness.

If the slab of concrete is an irregular shape, again, draw it to scale on graph paper with every square representing a given area, count the whole squares, work out the approximate area of the broken squares, and add them together to find the total surface area.

Metrication

Quantity	Multiply by:
Mass	
ounces to grams	28.3495
pounds to kilograms	0.4536
Volume	
fluid ounces to millilitres	28.413
pints to litres	0.5682
quarts to litres	1.1365
gallons (imperial) to litres	4.546
cubic feet to cubic metres	0.0283
cubic yards to cubic metres	0.7646
Length	
inches to millimetres	25.4
feet to metres	0.3048
yards to metres	0.9144
Areas	
square inches to square millimetres	645.16
square feet to square metres	0.0929
square yards to square metres	0.8361
morgen to hectares	0.8565
acres to hectares	0.4046

Handy formulae	
Area of a triangle	Base × ½ height
Area of a rectangle	Length × breadth
Circumference of a circle	Diameter × 3,1416
Volume of a cylinder	Base area × height
Volume of a cube	Length × breadth × height

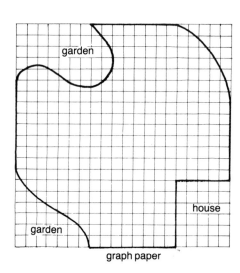

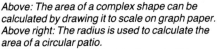

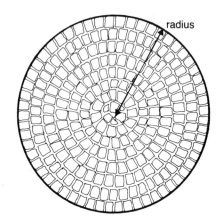

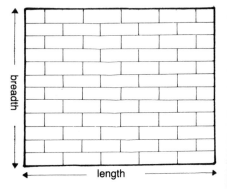

Above: The area of a complex shape can be calculated by drawing it to scale on graph paper.
Above right: The radius is used to calculate the area of a circular patio.
Right: Length x breadth gives the area of a rectangular patio.

Accurate measuring

All the building work you do in your garden – or elsewhere – should be 'square'. This means that every corner of a structure must be exactly 90° and a square should be precisely what the term denotes: square.

The mistake most do-it-yourselfers make is simply laying the bricks for a wall or patio in a line that looks more-or-less straight. The result is a crooked, unsightly wall or a patio whose bricks never had a chance of being laid in even, straight lines.

Always remember this great building truth: in bricklaying, you just cannot get a professional result unless everything is exactly level and square (at right angles). This is why a spirit level is the right hand of every professional bricklayer, and also why he insists that his builder's line is set up accurately before he lays the first brick.

For a smallish job, like laying a little concrete slab outside your kitchen door, an ordinary builder's square will usually be quite adequate to ensure that the corners are set out square. To save money, you can make your own out of wood. See how to do this on page 37.

For bigger projects, such as a square patio, or even the setting out of a garage, you should use the 3-4-5 method. This method relies on drawing one base line on the ground to represent one side of the corner. This line should never be moved and will serve as the base from which all four corners are measured.

Measure out a distance of three feet along your base line. Now measure a distance of four feet along the other arm of the corner and stretch your measuring tape between the three and four feet marks, adjusting the arm until you get a reading of exactly five feet. The corner formed between the three measurements will be exactly 90°. The sketch shows how easy it is to do.

At any rate, that is the theory. In the garden you have to plan things a bit differently, as it is not always possible to draw perfectly accurate, straight lines over rocks, clods and bumps on the ground.

What you have to do is knock two pegs into the ground and tie a builder's line between them, to indicate your base line. Measure a distance of three feet along this line and mark it with a felt-tipped pen.

About 4½ feet from this base line, knock a third peg into the ground near the point where the corner is to be. Extend the line or string to this peg (a nail hammered into the top of the peg makes a good attachment for the string) and ask somebody to stretch the string taut. Once again, the sketch shows how easily it is done. Measure a distance of four feet along the string and make a mark at this point.

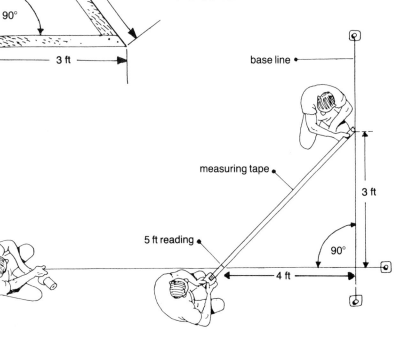

This is how to measure out a 90° angle on the ground. Make your own square from scrap timber (see also page 37). You can use any unit, for instance inches, provided the ratio remains 3:4:5.

Now hold the end of your measuring tape against the three-foot mark on the base line and stretch the tape diagonally across to the four-foot mark until you get a reading of five feet. Now your first corner is exactly square and the builder's line you have just set up will serve as the base line for your next corner.

Repeat the whole process with each of the three remaining corners. Bear in mind that the corners are determined by the points at which the lines cross each other and not by the positions of the pegs, which should always be erected about half a foot beyond the marks.

In the case of houses and outbuildings, L-shaped profile planks are used, and lines stretching from these indicate the positions of the outside boundaries of the foundations and the width of the walls. But you need not bother yourself with this. Suffice to say that the same principle – the 3-4-5 method – is used for laying a simple patio with right-angled corners.

Test

Because it is easy to make tiny measurement errors here and there (and a few inches' error at one corner can easily become a few feet over a long distance), you should always check that your corners are still square once you have set out all the builder's lines.

All you have to do is to get somebody to hold the end of your tape measure over the exact spot at which the two corner lines cross. Stretch the tape diagonally across to the other corner and mark the measurement with your thumb. Now transfer the tape to the other two corners and check the measurement. If your corners are square, the two diagonal measurements will be exactly the same.

If the two measurements do not agree, shift the position of the nails or pegs until you do get equal readings.

16. SYMBOLS FOR THE GARDEN PLAN

You can copy these symbols to help you with your final garden plan or colour in the parts you wish to use, and cut them out. Colour the lawn green and select naturalistic colours for trees, shrubs and so on. The brickwork can be brown, while the seats and other symbols can be in colours of your choice. See Chapter 2 for how to plan your garden accurately on paper.

concrete blocks with brick edging

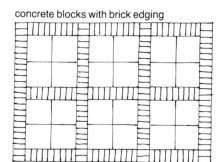

concrete paving slabs

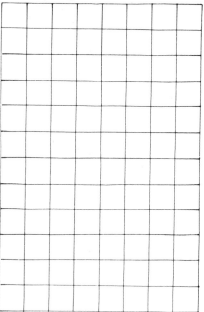

crazy paving

concrete paving blocks laid in grass

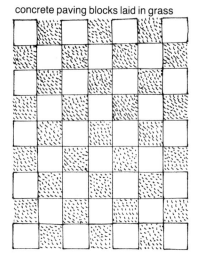

stepping stones

garden wall/edging

garden path/paving blocks

paths

steps

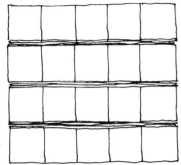

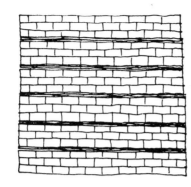

brick paving

shrub/ border/ garden

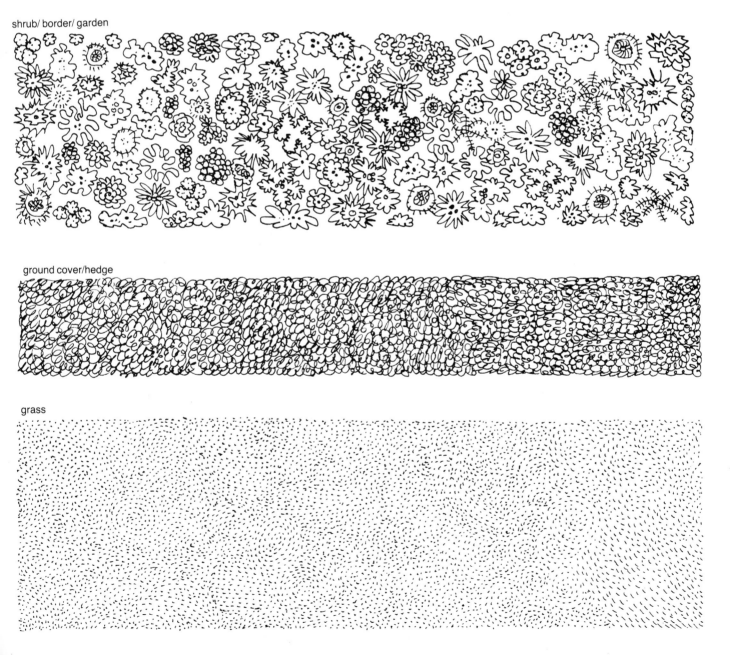

ground cover/hedge

grass

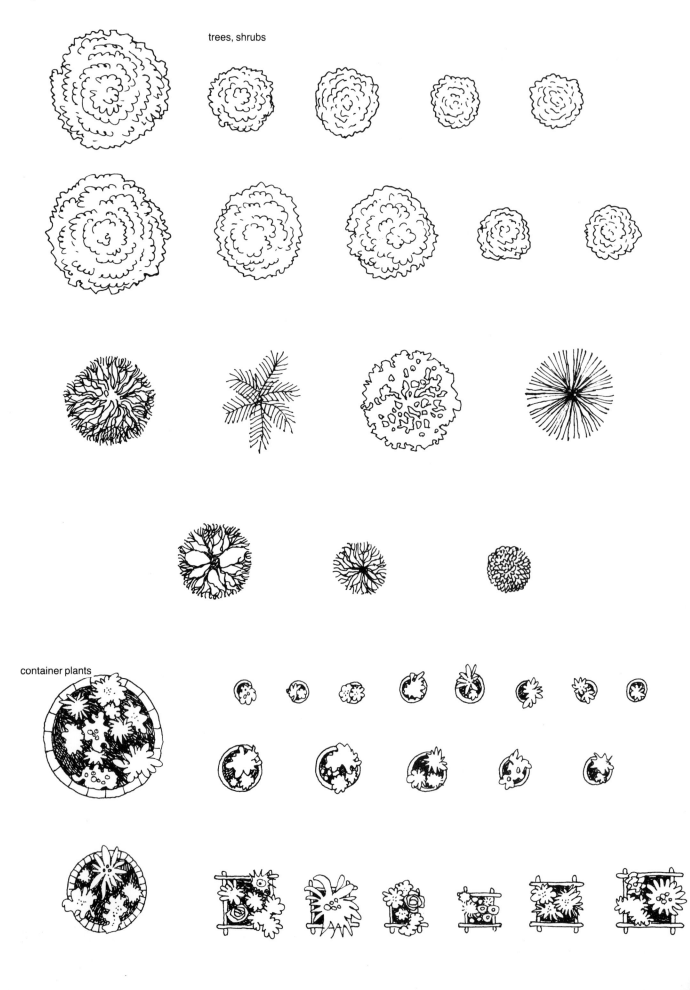

trees, shrubs

container plants

fish ponds

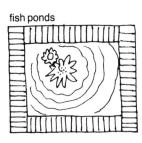

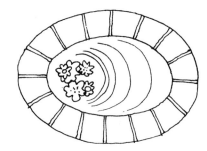

birdbath

barbecue with seating

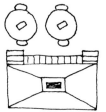

barbecue

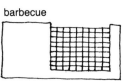

table with benches

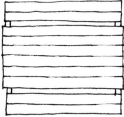

table with chairs

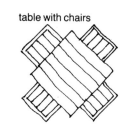

table and chairs

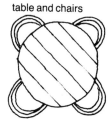

washing line

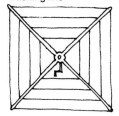

benches

Professional Associations:

American Concrete Institute
Box 19150
Redford Sta.
Detroit, Mi. 48219

Portland Cement Assoc.
5420 Old Orchard Rd.
Skokie, Il. 60077

Brick Institute of America
11490 Commerce Park Dr.
Suite 300
Reston, Va. 22091

American Society of Landscape
Architects
1733 Connecticut Ave., N.W.
Washington, D.C. 20009

National Association of Lawn and
Garden Manufacturers
Box 28279
1740 E. Joppa Rd.
Baltimore, Md. 21234

National Concrete Masonry Assoc.
2302 Horse Pen Rd.
Herndon, Va. 22070

Suppliers:

Masonry Specialty Co.
4430 Gibsonia Rd.
Gibsonia, Pa. 15044

Goldblatt Tool Co.
P.O. Box 2334, 511 Osage St.
Kansas City, Ks. 66110

Osmose Sunwood (Pressure Treated
Wood)
Osmose Wood Preserving, Inc.
980 Ellicott St.
Buffalo, N.Y. 14209